The Religious Imagi

THE RELIGIOUS IMAGINATION

by Andrew M. Greeley

Sadlier

Los Angeles   New York   Chicago

Acknowledgements

Lawrence Kubie. *Neurotic Distortion and the Creative Process*. New York: Farrar, Straus and Giroux, 1961.

Jacques Maritain. *Creative Intuition in Art and Poetry*. Vol. 1 of *The A. W. Mellon Lectures in the Fine Arts*, Bollingen Series XXXV. Copyright 1953 by the Trustees of the National Gallery of Art. Selections from pp. 48-49, 91-92, 94, 96, 98-99. Footnotes deleted. Reprinted by permission of Princeton University Press.

Library of Congress Catalog Card Number: 81-52855

ISBN: 0-8215-9876-7

Printed in the United States of America

Published by William H. Sadlier, Inc., 11 Park Place, New York, New York 10007

Contents

89137

The Religious Imagination

Highlights

1   *Religious imagination is an essential key to understanding human religious behavior.*

2   *Religion is a meaning system expressed in "symbols"—images that are prior to and perhaps more powerful than propositions. They and the meaning we give them constitute the religious imagination.*

3   *All religious symbols are implicitly narrative and merge with our own stories to give them meaning and purpose.*

4   *Human beings have a built-in propensity to hope and the capacity for experiences which renew their hope.*

5   *Certain realities are especially likely to trigger experiences of hope. These experiences are recorded first of all in the imagination.*

6   *Religion is an activity of that dimension of the human personality which may be called pre-conscious, poetic, or creative.*

7   *Religion becomes a communal event where persons are able to link their own grace experiences with the grace experiences of their religious tradition.*

8   *Our religious stories are basically stories of relationships.*

Chapter 1

The Religious Imagination

This book is about the importance of the religious imagination. While the religious imagination is prior to religious intellect psychologically and perhaps chronologically, the religious intellect is important for two reasons:

1. The human person is a unit. Imagination and intellect, while different in "dimensions" (for want of a better word) are nonetheless part of the same personality.

2. While the raw, elementary power of religion comes first through the imagination, it is the nature of human beings to reflect on their experience. Intellect examines experience, automatically and necessarily. It may be a long chronological and philosophical path from the apostles' experience on Easter Sunday and the residual images that experience left in their imagination to the Councils of Chalcedon and Ephesus some 400 years later. The philosophical categories articulated at those councils would surely not have been understood by either the apostles or the New Testament authors. Nevertheless, religious experience in creatures who are intellect as well as imagination inevitably leads to reflection, theology, philosophy, and creed. This is precisely because humans must examine their experiences and the images which resonate these experiences.

The emphasis here is on the social scientific study of the religious imagination because so little attention has been paid to the subject by social scientists and ecclesiastical thinkers and leaders. The typical social science study of religion focuses on denominational membership and affiliation, frequency of church attendance, and acceptance of certain doctrinal and ethical propositions. Yet human religious behavior can be much better understood by measuring (however crudely) the state of a respondent's religious imagination. Tell me what your image is of God, your picture of Jesus, your fantasy of an afterlife, and I will know a good deal more about you religiously than if I just know how often you go to church or whether you believe in papal infallibility.

As a graduate student and a young researcher, I was persuaded by the work of Clifford Geertz that a religion is a "meaning" system or a "culture" system, that is, an attempt by humans to deal with the complexities of life, indeed the ultimate complexities of life: questions of good and evil, tragedy and injustice, hope and love. Geertz, in his classic definition of religion, calls it 1) a system of symbols which acts to 2) establish powerful, pervasive, and long-lasting moods and motivations in people by 3) formulating conceptions of a general order of existence and 4) clothing these conceptions with such an aura of factuality that 5) the moods and motivations seem uniquely realistic.

In the early 1970s, with a generous grant from the Henry Luce Foundation, my colleague Professor William McCready and I began to investigate the possibility of using in empirical research Geertz's notion of religion as a meaning system. McCready reported the findings of this project in a book, *The Ultimate Values of the American Population*. He argued persuasively that the meaning system approach was a valid and useful way of looking at religion. Subsequently, however, we both decided that we had been too propositional. We had presented our respondents with pictures, indeed, vignettes of life situations—the prospect of one's own imminent death, the birth of a handicapped child, and others—but we had attempted to measure propositional responses to these situations. Later it seemed to us that when Geertz said "symbols" he meant pictures and images which were prior to and perhaps more powerful than propositions. In the meantime I read theology books by David Tracy, John Shea, and Nathan Scott which heavily emphasized the importance of religious "story" as anterior to and more powerful than religious doctrine. These stories were rooted in religious experiences or, as Tracy calls them, "limit experiences." At the same time, McCready and I reanalyzed materials collected in the Luce Foundation study about religious experiences. We were deeply impressed with the proportion of the American population (almost two-fifths) which had powerful religious experiences of the sort described by William James, and by the impact of these experiences on the lives of those who had them.

Toward the end of the 1970s, many American social scientists became interested in "narrative models." Sociologists like Goffmann and Garfinkel, psychologists working with computer simulations of human intelligence, anthropologists like Geertz, and even political scientists like Kenneth Prewitt, the present President of the Social Science Research Council, have all argued in different ways that "narrative" or "story" is minimally a useful model for analyzing human behavior. Perhaps more than that, it may also be a model that is structured into the nature of human beings, whatever that might be. We might well enjoy telling stories and listening to them because we are all the storytellers who narrate accounts of our own life.

What theologians like Tracy and Shea and philosophers like Paul Ricoeur were doing in their attempts to interpret religion, social scientists were doing in their attempts to understand broader dimensions of human behavior. It occurred to me, particularly after reading the brilliant work of John Shea, that all religious symbols are implicitly narrative, that they tell a story of the meaning of human life and especially the meaning of a particular human life which is in process. Religious stories merge with our own stories to give them meaning and purpose. To some extent religious stories give our stories shape and direction. Geertz's original insight that religion was a set of meaning-bestowing symbols now meant more to me than it had previously. The symbols had to be pictures and images before they became propositions, and they also had to be implicitly narrative. (Whether all symbols tell stories or not is a matter beyond the scope of this book. Religious symbols do, however, and I believe necessarily so.)

I have attempted to organize and articulate my reflections upon religion as experience and religion as story in a book called *Religion: A Secular Theory*. At the same time I was writing that volume I was engaged in a study of young Catholic adults for the Knights of Columbus, a Catholic fraternal organization. My colleagues for this research were McCready, Teresa Sullivan, and Joan Fee. The study provided an opportunity to test the theoretical propositions I was formulating. The present book is an empirical study of the religious imagination which tests, in part at least, the theory set down in *Religion: A Secular Theory*. Five different NORC surveys are used in my analysis. Although the material from the Young Catholic Adult Study is the richest of the data sources available to me, I would emphasize that this is not a report of that study. Two formal reports of that study have been published elsewhere. The material in them is not duplicated in this volume. The Knights of Columbus, the Luce Foundation, and the other funding agencies are not responsible for the theoretical speculation or the empirical interpretation of the data provided in the present volume.

I also wish to emphasize that my "model" of religion, presented in some considerable detail in *Religion: A Secular Theory* and tested in the present volume is not by any means intended to be an exclusive model of human religious behavior. It is offered merely as a useful perspective for looking at religion, useful for both ordering empirical data and, I am prepared to contend, for making religious "policy." A prominent Catholic ecclesiastic, reading a version of some of my material, complained that the treatment was "too empirical" and did not leave enough "room for God and the Holy Spirit." I dealt only with the psychological and the sociological, he contended, and not with the contribution of faith.

I would disagree, for I am convinced that it is only within religious image that one finds the basic raw material of faith. While I am not a theologian and this is not a theology book, it is my understanding that good Catholic theology sees God operating, normally at least, through "secondary" causes; that is to say, God works on creatures through other creatures, presumably through other human creatures. How these other humans can have their effect except through social action escapes me completely. Therefore I am convinced that my model does indeed leave room for the working of the Spirit. In fact, if pushed into a corner, I would argue that it leaves more room than almost any other social scientific model of religion I know. It is, however, no more than a model. It provisionally and partially provides a crude and necessarily inadequate perspective for examining religious behavior and for proposing religious policy.

I intend to present the evidence in this book as a sociologist. I will make no judgments within the pages of the book as to whether the "stories of God" told in the religious imagery I am studying are ultimately true or false, revealing or deceptive, sacramental or wish-fulfilling. This "agnosticism" is methodological, not theological. Empirical social science can only study human religious behavior and the images which relate with this behavior. It cannot, on the basis of its own data, say whether there is a "reality," much less a "Reality," that corresponds to the pictures that have somehow been generated in the religious imagination. If I make policy suggestions in this book (particularly for the Catholic Church because so much of the data on which the book is based deals with Catholics), I do so from the purely sociological viewpoint. They are the kind of recommendations, I think, that a non-Catholic, even a non-believing sociologist, might make from the same or similar analyses.

If the reader wishes to raise the question of whether I believe the "stories of God" and the "stories of faith" (the titles of Shea's two books) that are incarnated in the religious imagery I am studying, my response is that of course I believe them. But this is not a book about my beliefs or my theology—or about anyone's theology. It is a book about the stories of God that can be found in the religious imagination of American Catholics, particularly young American Catholics, and the implications of these stories for the presumably nonreligious dimensions of their lives.

I now turn to a brief summary of my model of religion, a précis in effect of a longer statement to be found in *Religion: A Secular Theory*:

1. *Human nature has a built-in propensity to hope.* Whether that hope is genetically programmed, as Lionel Tiger has argued, or merely a powerful psychological need, is not pertinent for my theory. It is sufficient to say that in McCready's research more than four-fifths of the American people gave hopeful or optimistic responses to potentially tragic situations. Death research, resuscitation research, game analysis all demonstrate this powerful and persistent tendency of humans to hope even when the situation seems hopeless, even when they can find no specific content to their hope.

2. *Humans also have the capacity for experiences which renew their hope.* These experiences may for some people be the spectacular experience of which William James wrote in his *Varieties of Religious Experience*, about which McCready and I in the United States and Sir Alistair Hardy, David Hay, and Ann Morissey in Great Britain have done research. (Eighty percent of Americans have some kind of hope-renewing experience in their lives.) These experiences may also be much less spectacular—a desert sunset, a touch of a friendly hand, a reconciliation after a quarrel, the grin on the face of a toddler, solving of an ethical or mathematical problem, even a good night's sleep. Experiences like this, as David Tracy points out in his book, *A Blessed Rage for Order*, are experiences of "gratuity," wonderful events which did not have to happen but did. We encounter with them the limitations of our existence (Tracy calls them "limit-" or "horizon-experiences") which also confirm that, despite those limitations, our existence is "gifted," something that did not have to happen, did not have to be—yet is. It is not clear whether there is simply one kind of "limit-experience" with different degrees of intensity or whether there are a wide variety of such experiences. What matters for the purpose of my theory is that such experiences occur with varying degrees of intensity in virtually everyone's life, providing hints of purpose, "rumors of angels," intimations of . . . something, encounters with "otherness."

The "otherness" is diffuse and amorphous, but, with some exceptions (the horror experience of Bergman's spider, for example, in his film *Through a Glass Darkly)*, suggests or hints at some purpose in our existence which is beyond that existence. For my purposes, that is all that needs be said. I contend that the origins of religion are to be found in such hints. The origins of religious traditions are to be found in massive hints, such as the apostles' Easter experience, and the origin—psychological if not chronological and biographical—that individual humans' personal religion is rooted in their own hint of personal gratuity. Creatures born with the propensity to hope, we are confirmed in that propensity by certain "encounters" in our lives. That which is "encountered" is most often experienced simply as "otherness" but on occasion, or frequently for some people, it can be a powerful, demanding, passionately loving "otherness." Hence, on reflection, we speak of the "otherness" as "The Other." Both historically and psychologically I believe this to be the origin first of the image and then of the concept of "God."

Philosophically, an examination of religion may well begin with the question of whether God exists (a question which has been brilliantly addressed recently by Professor Hans Kung), but humanly, the experience of gratuity and the encounter with The Other precedes the question of whether God exists (though most of us, of course, come to our limit-experience with an existing notion of God, a notion which may or may not fit that which we experience). However, both the God concept and the God issue are derivative. The more fundamental and primordial question is whether reality is such as to guarantee the propensity to hope: Is reality truly that which we experience in our interludes of hopefulness? John MacQuarrie, an English theologian, put the question nicely when he said that the primary question is whether reality (or Reality) is gracious (or Gracious). From the point of view of the social scientist that is also the basic question. What are the stories that reveal reality as gracious? What impact do such stories have on a person's life?

What should these hope-rewarding experiences be called? Tracy calls them "limit-experiences," John Shea calls them "experiences of mystery," Rudolph Otto calls them "encounters with the Holy," Peter Berger says they are "rumors of angels," others call them "signals of the transcendent." I choose to call them *experiences of grace* because the term "grace" has an ancient and honorable history and because these experiences of wonder, mystery, or gratuity all hint that our hope is justified by "otherness" which is also "loving goodness." Just as a "gracious" hostess is charming, concerned, attractive, affectionate, so the "otherness" encountered in hope-rewarding experiences seems to be "gracious." In this book my term "experience of grace" describes those experiences which renew and reinvigorate human hopefulness. I hasten to add that I do not use the word "grace" necessarily in any theological sense; I will leave to theologians the discussion of whether my usage and theirs might come to the same. Nor am I asserting that there is a reality lurking beyond the experience that reality is "graceful" or even "Graceful." I am merely asserting that the vast majority of humans have experiences which suggest that the "graceful" or "Graceful" may lurk somewhere out there. Such encounters may account, if not for the existence of human religion, at least for its power and persistence.

FIGURE 1.1

**General Model to
Explain Religious Imagination**

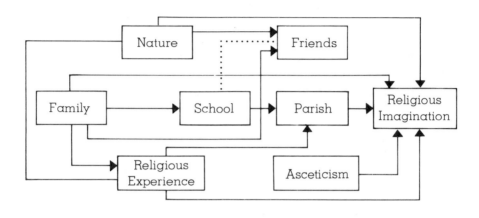

3. While any reality may trigger a grace experience (and hence everything is sacramental in the sense that everything has the potentiality of revealing the source of our hopefulness), *there are certain realities which because of their power, their importance, or their prevalence are especially likely to trigger such experiences* (and hence are sacraments par excellence): fire, the sun, water, the moon, oil, love, sex, marriage, death, community. For reasons of biology, psychology, or culture, these realities seem especially likely to trigger grace experiences for many human beings.

The Jewish Passover, for example, recapitulates three different pre-Sinai pagan spring festivals, all resonating with the fertility of spring: the unleavened bread festival of an agricultural people, the paschal lamb festival of a pastoral people, and the fire and water festival of the more sophisticated urban people. The Christian passover absorbed these powerful and ancient symbolisms and articulated more sharply the fire and water symbolism by absorbing a more explicit intercourse rite, plunging the fiery candle (the male organ) into the life-giving water (the female organ), which originated in Roman fertility rites. We can leave to psychologists and historians of religion explanations of both the power and the persistence of such symbolism. Here it need only be noted that they stir up deep resonances in the human imagination.

9

4. *The experience is recorded first of all in that aspect of the personality we normally call "the imagination."* The experience of grace, first of all, is an impact on the senses and then is filtered through the imagination where it has an enormous and sometimes overwhelming effect. Even long after the experience is over the residue remains in the imagination, capable of recollection and of exciting once again resonances of the experience. The interaction between experience and imagination is complex and intricate. The repertory of images and pictures available to any given person's or community's imagination will respond to the experience and shape of both the perception and the recollection of the experience, if not the experience itself. Thus the apostles' Easter experience of Jesus not dead but alive was encoded in the imagery of contemporary Judaism. Jesus as Moses, Jesus as Adam, Jesus as prophet, as Messiah, even as "resurrected," was experienced in accordance with the "story" common in Pharisaic Judaism. All these images or "stories" were part of the imaginative repertory available to the followers of Jesus. Their experience of Jesus perceived as alive (and for the purposes of the present volume I am only concerned with the historical fact of such an experience and not with its religious or theological interpretation) triggered such images and pictures. The images and pictures shaped the experience, or at least the resonance to it. In the process the images, pictures, and stories were themselves transformed so that they meant something rather different to the apostles afterwards, when they tried to describe the experience. Jesus was "like" a new Adam, and yet there was more to be said because the Adam "story" had been changed as a result of the Easter experience.

5. *Religion is an activity of that dimension of the human personality which may be called preconscious or poetic or creative.* Michael Polanyi, in the closing years of his remarkable life, wrote extensively on personal knowledge or tacit knowledge; that is, the deeply insightful, intuitive cognition that we have about things before we "know" them in any self-conscious and explicit fashion. According to Polanyi, our great discoveries come not as clearly thought-out answers to carefully prepared questions based on theoretical consideration according to the standard format of the "scientific method." On the contrary, the great insights, the "paradigm-shattering ones," to use the phrase of Thomas Kuhn, come before the answers and even before the questions. At some deep level in our personalities we intuit the truth about reality, and then, under the influence of this intuition, seek to ask the questions which will enable us to "surface" our insight as an articulated answer to the questions. This description of personal knowledge flies in the face of all we learned in our high school and college textbooks about scientific method.

Claude Levi-Strauss, in his discussions of symbolic myths, speaks of the French "artistic game" of *bricollage*. The artist or craftsman, working with a limited set of components—some string, a few rocks, some pieces of wood, some bits of wire—assembles, demolishes, and then reassembles constructs which can represent as many different things as his playful imagination wants to make them represent. Levi-Strauss suggests that the myth-makers operate in the same way. They have a limited number of images, pictures, metaphors, stories, symbols, and they endlessly rearrange, reconstruct, reorder their component parts into similar and yet diverse myths in much the same way our dreams rearrange the experiences of our waking conscious life. It is clear that tellers of folk tales enjoy tremendous liberty in manipulating their limited resources to make many different, though not unrelated, points about the meaning of the human condition. Homer, for example, must have relied on a vast collection of divergent folk tales which in a work of sheer genius he wove into a seamless web. In Irish mythology the tales of Finn MacCool and of Queen Maeve are by no means part of a single well-integrated story (though sometimes attempts were made in the old sagas to force the divergent tales together), but are rather the creations of different storytellers with different goals and purposes.

The same bricollage phenomenon is at work in both the Jewish and Christian Scriptures. The book of Tobit, for example, is clearly composed of a number of folk tales and folk images that were "lying around" for the teller of the tale just as the pieces of string and wire and wood were "lying around" in a French farmyard. More importantly, the late apocalyptic literature of the Second Temple era was put together in substantial part by reweaving the Creation myths found in Genesis but certainly existing long before the writing of Genesis, into Hebrew folk mythology. So too even in the Christian Scriptures there is no single account of the death of Jesus and no single discription of his followers' experience of him as still alive. Instead, many different tales and traditions have emerged making rather different points by the manipulation of the various components of pictures and stories.

Mihaly Czikszentmihalyi has developed the notion of "flow" to describe certain "peak" experiences of altered or quasi-altered states of consciousness. It is the nature of "flow" experience to push our talents and our skills to their outer limits, but not beyond those limits. The chess player faced with a difficult opponent, but one with whom he is well-matched; the surgeon, performing intricate operations that are just inside the limits of his abilities; the skier, negotiating a tricky slope that he knows he can master; the quarterback, "reading" the defensive secondary—all these experience "flow" states. Their disciplined, highly trained, carefully-polished skills react quickly, automatically, smoothly, responding with casual decisiveness to every slight movement in the situation. It is as though the skills themselves take over and direct the person involved.

John Brodie, who once tossed a football for the San Francisco '49ers, described such an experience as a "slow motion" drama in which he could see his responses to the slowly unfolding defensive patterns even before he had responded. His skills as quarterback, in other words, "told him" what to do without his having to devote any conscious thought to the problem, let us say, of a free safety leaving his position and crossing the field. Similarly, trial lawyers—or anyone else who must think on his/her feet—often describe their responses in critical situations as words they themselves never would have "thought" of if they had time. The words just came; they "flowed" out of them.

What exactly goes on in this altered state of consciousness? What is the nature of this "creative" process? Does a muse, indeed, take over and whisper in our ear, as some varieties of Platonic philosophy once suggested? Today that seems an absurd question, and yet the poet, the artist, the painter, I think, will all testify that they do "hear" voices or do "see" visions. The model of a "muse" nicely subsumes the data.

The creative process, in other words, seems to be something intellectual, but intellectual in a quite different way than our ordinary thought process is intellectual. Aristotle postulated an "active" or "agent" intellect, a dimension of the human personality, if you will, which not only received knowledge, but actively "went out" to order the components from which knowledge would come. The Islamic Aristotelians in Spain in the early Middle Ages were so impressed by the power of the *intellectus agens* that they suggested that there was but a single such intellect for the whole human race in which we all participated—a construct not at all unlike, in the last analysis, the Platonic muse. Most Platonists and some Aristotelians, then, were so impressed with the power that takes over in the altered state of consciousness called creativity that they placed this power outside the human personality. Thomas Aquinas, stable, sensible Neapolitan that he was, dismissed such a notion, and the creative intellect was put back where it belonged—solidly within the personality of the ordinary individual—even if it was still seen as a spark of some higher Creativity.

If, therefore, creativity is neither in the daily consciousness, nor in the Freudian unconsciousness, nor in some Platonic or Aristotelian hyperconsciousness, where else is it? One runs out of prefixes and ends up with the notion of the preconscious. In the last several decades two very different individuals developed from very different traditions the notion of the preconscious intellect as the locus of human creativity: the psychoanalyst Lawrence Kubie (in his book *Neurotic Distortion and the Creative Process)* and the Thomistic philosopher Jacques Maritain (in the A. W. Mellon Lectures in the Fine Arts at the National Gallery of Arts). This strange convergence of the psychoanalyst and the philosopher—of which the two men were apparently totally unaware—is a fascinating phenomenon, and while convergence does not "prove" the existence of a preconscious intellect, it does lend some plausibility to the model.

Be it noted, by the way, that one is dealing here with a model, a postulate to explain phenomena, rather than a clearly proven dimension of the human personality.

First let us listen to Lawrence Kubie. He places the preconscious of the human personality between the rational and the unconscious.

> There is, however, another type of mentation whose relationship to its roots is figurative and allegorical. The function of this intermediate form of mentation is to express at least by implication the nuances of thought and feeling, those collateral and emotional references which cluster around the central core of meaning. Here every coded signal has many overlapping meanings, and every item of data from the world of experience has many coded representatives. This is the form of coded language which is essential for all creative thinking, whether in art or science. Therefore, we will have much more to say about it below. In technical jargon, this second type of symbolic process is called *preconscious*
>
> . . . On the conscious level he (a scientist) deals with them as communicable ideas and approximate realities. On the *preconscious* level he deals with swift condensations of their multiple allegorical and emotional import, both direct and indirect. On the *unconscious* level, without realizing it, he uses his special competence and knowledge to express the conflict-laden and confused levels of his own spirit, using the language of his specialty as a vehicle for the outward projection of his own internal struggles. Since this happens without his knowledge, it is a process which even in his own field can take over his creative thinking, distorting and perverting it to serve his unconscious needs and purposes, precisely as happens in a dream or in the symptom formations of neurotic and psychotic illness.

Caught as it is between ordinary waking consciousness and the unconscious, the preconscious is in trouble.

Preconscious processes are assailed from both sides. From one side they are nagged and prodded into rigid and distorted symbols by unconscious drives which are oriented away from reality and which consist of rigid compromise formations, lacking in fluid inventiveness. From the other side they are driven by literal conscious purpose, checked and corrected by conscious retrospective critique. The uniqueness of creativity, i.e., its capacity to find and put together something new, depends on the extent to which preconscious functions can operate freely between these two ubiquitous concurrent and oppressive prison wardens.

Finally, Kubie believed that the preconscious exercise of creativity is essentially a matter of seeing new relations—a bricollage exercise, in other words.

It is, I believe, a fair generalization to state quite simply that although the uncovering of new facts and of new relationships among both new and old data is not the whole of creativity, it is the essential process without which there can be no such thing as creativity. Consequently, creativity implies *invention*; e.g., the making of new machines or processes by the application of old or new facts and principles or a combination of them in order to uncover still newer facts and newer combinations, and to synthesize new patterns out of data whose interdependence had hitherto gone unnoted and unused. It is this which is common to all creativeness, whether in music as described by Mozart, or in painting as described by Delacroix and others, or in poetry as described by Paul Valéry, A. E. Housman, etc., or in science as pointed out by Gregg, Claude Bernard, Richard Tolman, Richet, and other scientists.

Incidentally, later in the book Kubie compares preconscious activity to that of music—a comparison that he, without realizing it, has in common with both Plato and Maritain: "The extraordinary power of preconscious condensation is often demonstrated by a single thought which reverberates through the mind like a haunting melody."

Now to turn to Jacques Maritain. Creativity, "art," as Maritain calls it, is a "habitus, an inner quality or stable and deep rooted disposition that raises the human subject and his natural powers to a higher degree of vital formation and energy, making him possessed of a particular strength of his own . . . a master quality, an inner demon if you prefer—has developed in us . . . (and) is an ennoblement in the very kingdom of human nature and human dignity."

Creativity, then, is or at least involves, first of all the disciplined skill. Nor is it to be found either outside the human personality or in the depths of the human unconscious. It is in

> " . . . neither the surrealist inferno nor the Platonic heaven. I think that what we have to do is to make the Platonic Muse descend into the soul of man, where she is no longer Muse, but creative intuition; and Platonic inspiration descend into the intellect united with imagination . . . (nor) is it a purely unconscious activity . . . but, rather . . . an activity which is *principally* unconscious, but, the point of which emerges into consciousness. Poetic intuition, for instance, is born in the unconscious, but it emerges from it; the poet is not unaware of this intuition, on the contrary it is his most precious light and the primary rule of his virture . . . . But, he is aware of it . . . on the *edge* of the unconscious." (Author's italics)

Maritain concludes:

> There are two kinds of unconscious, two great domains of psychological activity screened from the grasp of consciousness: the preconscious of the spirit in its living springs, and the unconscious of blood and flesh, instincts, tendencies, complexes, repressed images and desires, traumatic memories, as constituting a closed or autonomous dynamic whole. I would like to designate the first kind of unconscious by the name of *spiritual* or, for the sake of Plato, *musical* unconscious or preconscious; and the second by the name of *automatic* unconscious or *deaf* unconscious—deaf to the intellect, and structured into a world of its own apart from the intellect; we might also say, in quite a general sense, leaving aside any particular theory, *Freudian unconscious*. (Author's italics)

Note how almost miraculously similar are the comments of Maritain and Kubie even in the reference to music. Maritain insists that this creative activity is an activity of reason, but he defines reason to include something much broader then ordinary waking consciousness. (Incidentally, Maritain has a diagram on page 108 of his book, and Kubie, on page 40, which are strikingly similar in their contents, if not their graphics.)

> Reason does not only consist of its conscious logical tools and manifestations, nor does the will consist only of its deliberate conscious determinations. Far beneath the sunlit surface thronged with explicit concepts and judgments, words and expressed resolutions or movements of the will, are the sources of knowledge and

creativity, of love and suprasensuous desires, hidden in the primordial trans-lucid night of the intimate vitality of the soul. Thus, it is that we must recognize the existence of an unconscious or preconscious which pertains to the spiritual powers of the human soul and to the inner abyss of personal freedom, and of the personal thirst and striving for knowing and seeing, grasping and expressing; a spiritual or musical unconscious which is specifically different from the automatic or deaf unconscious.

Maritain goes beyond Kubie to give a name to the functioning preconscious. He calls it the "Agent Intellect" or the "Illuminating Intellect." It is that part of our personality which analyzes and decomposes reality outside. It serves it up for the consideration of our conscious, rational, discursive mind. It is "a merely active and perpetually active intellectual energy . . . which permeates the images with its pure and purely activating spiritual life and actuates or awakens the potential intelligibility which is contained in them." It is that energy which operates on the images gathered by our sense, drawing the intelligible content from these images. "The Illuminating Intellect is spiritual sun ceaselessly radiating, which activates everything in intelligence, and whose light causes all our ideas to arise in us, and whose energy permeates every operation of our mind. And this primal source of light cannot be seen by us; it remains concealed in the unconscious of the spirit."

Maritain suggests that the preconscious—the locus of creativity—is in fact a ceaselessly operating intellectual energy which is an essential part of the human act of knowing. Our images can either be in the automatic unconscious of Freud or in the spiritual preconscious; and it is precisely insofar as they are in the spiritual preconscious that they present the raw material of creativity. For those who may be tempted to dismiss Maritain as a reactionary Thomist, one can only point out that he is saying virtually the same thing as is the American psychoanalyst, Lawrence Kubie. Both situate the source of creativity in a "scanning mechanism" locked in the depths of the human personality, but operating beyond the depths, ceaselessly exploring like a searchlight or radar antennae the world outside, and "locking on" to that world through the pictures and images it uncovers. The creative activity of the preconscious, freed temporarily from the constraint of literal reason, "takes over," releases our deeply intuitive personal knowledge, activates the smooth flow of our skills, and rearranges the components with which we are playing.

It is in the process something like this that I am suggesting that the religious imagination produces the symbols which resonate with the reality that has been experienced. Obviously at the present state of our knowledge it is impossible empirically to test, at least directly, such an assumption. However, as will be seen later on in this book, propositions based on the assumption do, indeed, stand up to empirical validation.

The purpose of religious discourse is not to communicate doctrinal propositions, but rather to stir up in the other person resonances of experiences similar to that which the religious storyteller himself or herself has had. Thus the telling each year in Holy Week of the story of the death and resurrection of Jesus, complete with all the profoundly resonating liturgical imagery, is not designed primarily to communicate doctrinal propositions but to rekindle memories of death-rebirth experiences that have marked the lives of the hearers and to link those resonances to the historic experience of Christians through the ages, leading back to the founding experience itself. The Easter story, in other words, is primarily designed to rekindle memories of grace experiences and link them with overarching memories in the historical tradition. Religion as story leaps from imagination to imagination, and only then, if at all, from intellect to intellect.

6. *Religion becomes a communal event when a person is able to link his own grace experience with the overarching experience of his religious tradition* (or a religious tradition), that is to say, when he perceives a link between his experience of grace and the tradition's experience of grace when he becomes aware that there is a correspondence or a correlation between the resonating picture or story in his imagination and the story passed on by his religious heritage. Till that point the experience of grace is a private event, one which is not perceived as linked to anything that is formally known as religion. However, given the fact that most of us are products of a religious heritage, there is a tendency to resonate to our experiences in and through the images that we inherited from our tradition. Our own experiences of grace give an inchoate meaning to the story of our lives; they hint at purposes which exist beyond ourselves; they suggest that the story of our life, which has a beginning, a middle, and a trajectory toward conclusion, may well have a gracious purpose. Articulated with and resonating together with stories of our religious heritage, these personalized religious stories constitute a fundamental theme, a basic *leitmotif* which underpins and validates our own existence. They now have become a set of symbols which Geertz refers to in the definition of religion I quoted earlier.

We are all aware that we are storytellers, playing the leading role in the story that is our own life. Even if some philosophers insist that our life is a series of random events, we perceive life events linked through a number of basic themes within the context of beginning, middle, and thrust toward conclusion. One of the basic themes, I contend, is religious or ultimate; it is the theme, or if you will, the subplot, of the narration of our life which gives it final meaning by linking it on the one hand to our own experiences of grace and, on the other hand, to the overarching story themes of our religious heritage.

7. Finally, *just as the story of anyone's life is a story of relationships—so each person's religious story is a story of relationships.* (We walked the hills of Galilee and Jerusalem with *him* and knew *he* was special, but did not know just how special *he* was.) The principal sacraments in our lives are other human beings or, more precisely, our relationships with other human beings. While nonhuman objects, such as fire, water, sunset, and mountain, may stir up experiences of grace, loving goodness is mostly perceived through relationships with other humans. We are the principal sacrament, the principal sign, the principal symbols through which other persons encounter grace and hope validated, just as they are the principal sacrament, the meaning base, and validating hope for us. Ultimate loving goodness, if it does indeed reveal itself, seems to reveal itself mostly through proximate loving goodness.

Therefore, the religious imagination, which contains in free-floating imagery and story the religious subplot of our life, will, on the one hand, have considerable effect on how we behave toward other human beings and will, on the other hand, have been shaped to a considerable extent by our experiences with other human beings. The stories of grace both shape our sacramental encounters with others and have been shaped by prior sacramental encounters with others. It is this notion which I propose to examine in the subsequent chapters of this book.

Relationships at school, with friends, and with one's parish community, and eventually with one's spouse, make a powerful contribution to the shaping of one's religious imagination, a contribution which may be reinforced if one engages in additional ascetical practices, such as retreats, days of recollection, spiritual reading. Figure 1.1(page 9) represents graphically this guiding perspective. A person's religious imagination will be shaped to some extent by all the factors to the left of religious imagination in the diagram. The better, the warmer, the more satisfying the relationship implied in each one of the boxes in my chart, the more benign, the more gracious, the more hopeful will be the religious imagination of the person involved in such relationships. One may not expect, in the language of social science, to totally explain the religious imagination of anyone, especially since the measures we are dealing with are crude and the reality is intricate and complex. Professor Sidney Verba once remarked, "Reality is an R of .3." Social scientists are content with a model that explains about 10 percent of the variance. (The R^2 of .3 is .09.) They hope for more, dream for more, and sometimes expect more explanatory power out of their models, but social and human reality is far more intricate than that dealt with by the physical, chemical, or mathematical sciences.

To conclude and summarize this preliminary chapter, let us look at a grace experience that is both utterly secular and profoundly religious. This experience was shared with an enormous number of Americans by the choreographer and motion picture director, Bob Fosse. His encounter with grace was a death, or more precisely, a near-death experience which obviously had a shattering impact on his imagination. It would appear that in trying to make sense of the experience and the ecstatic joy which seemed to have come at the very point of his death, Fosse turned to the early literature on death and dying by Elisabeth Kübler-Ross and found that her description of the phases that precede death—denial, anger, bargaining, resurrection, and hope—corresponded to what happened to him. The five phases structured the dazzling, appalling, frightening, and exhilarating film, *All That Jazz*, in which Fosse's imagination, working frantically and feverishly (with remarkable artistic skills, be it noted) tries to share with us his experience of grace at the turning point of life by calling forth memories, resonances, of experience we have had. If the framework for the movie is Kübler-Ross' phases, the story line is what Catholics used to call "the particular judgment" in which Fosse reviews his life with the Angel of Death and, while there is yet time, expresses sorrow, contrition, and atonement. If he survives, he will at least try to do better. Then in the final phase, at the end, Fosse participates in his own "farewell" television show in which "all that jazz," which is his life, is scathingly reviewed. But the dazzling choreography is not despairing; it is hopeful. At the end, to the applause of all the characters that have been a part of his life, Fosse trips up the stairs, out of the TV studio and runs down the long corridor toward the light. Waiting for him there is "Angelique," the Angel of Death, dressed in filmy bridal clothes, smiling warmly as she welcomes Fosse/Gideon into their nuptial chamber.

The Kübler-Ross theme is heavily delineated in *All That Jazz*; the traditional religious themes are not nearly so clear, in the sense that one is not certain that Fosse realizes how heavily his imagination has been influenced by the Western religious heritage. Whatever one may think of the mixture of religion and explicit eroticism, the fundamental theme of *All That Jazz* is fundamentally Christian because it deals with death and resurrection, contrition and atonement, with love, hate, and love again. Fosse's dramatic artistic leap in which death/life is converted into a loving and lovely blond is authentic to tradition

19

which has always argued that death would finally consummate our nuptials with God. Christian theologians have been nervous with the implication that for men this turns God into the "fair bride" of which the book of Revelations speaks. From the theological viewpoint it is proper for the Church or for the human "soul" to be feminine, but God must be masculine—a perspective which may make the heavenly nuptials somewhat less attractive for men than for women. The great mystics of the Christian heritage have been much more explicit about the eroticism of intense union with the Ultimate. Fosse, perhaps without realizing it, shows us the route of mystics instead of the route of the theologians. Fortunate man, he seems to be innocent of technical theology.

In any event, *All That Jazz* is a spectacular "religious story" of a spectacular experience of grace, told by a man with relentless, resourceful, and extraordinary creative imagination. If we discount Fosse's pyrotechnic brillance and restless flair, we recognize that he depicts an experience we have shared. *All That Jazz* is a paradigm of this theory of the religious imagination. It shows a gratuitous experience of goodness, which renews hope, which creates a powerful impact on the imagination, leaves resonances which linger long after, and almost demands to be shared with others—not by teaching them doctrinal propositions but by telling them stories that resonate in their own imaginations.

Furthermore, it is a story (R rating or not) of the fair bride, a messenger of hope and grace who waits at the end of the tunnel to convert death into life.

Chapters two through ten of this book will report the origins, development, and impact of the religious imagination. The remaining chapters will deal with certain problems and opportunities which face the Church in the 1980s—teenagers, women, celibacy, the family, minority subcultures, out of wedlock unions—in the context of the implications these problems have on our theory on the religious imagination.

Measuring the Religious Imagination

Highlights

1   *In national surveys, both men and women were found to have warm and positive images of both Jesus and Mary (Table 2.1).*

2   *The majority of respondents pictured heaven as a life of peace, a spiritual life involving mind but not body, a place of intellectual communion with God and with loved ones.*

3   *The respondents looked at God the Father in less positive ways than they looked at Jesus and Mary. They tended to think of God in harsh images such as judge and master, rather than as lover.*

4   *A grace scale was developed which described a very warm, positive, and gracious view of the story of God and the individual. This scale also looked at the future as a place of action and pleasure which improves upon but does not negate our present life.*

5   *The "grace" scale indicates a very warm, positive, gracious view of the story of God and the individual as well as a future of action and pleasure which improves upon but does not negate our present life.*

Chapter 2

Measuring the Religious Imagination

This chapter will consist of a description of the construction of our measures of the religious imagination and the use of these measures to present a profile of the religious imagination of young Catholics. It should be remembered that the research being described is preliminary. This is the first attempt to measure the religious imagination and, therefore, our efforts are necessarily tentative and exploratory.

Each of the four questions presented in Figure 2.1 (page 24) constitutes, in effect, a matrix with a column of descriptive adjectives or nouns on the side of the matrix and a row of agreement categories across the top of the matrix. Thus in the question of Jesus there are 36 possible answers to the question, 9 adjectives with 4 categories of agreement. Of these 36 different cells in the matrix, the respondent is asked to choose 9. These choices constitute, in effect, a profile of the respondent's reaction to the person of Jesus (at least as that person might be described by 9 adjectives). The 9 adjectives describing Jesus, the 9 adjectives describing Mary, 10 nouns describing heaven and 8 nouns describing God constitute 4 matrices (or one giant matrix, if a person combines them) with 36 items and 4 response categories, or 144 possible responses, of which a respondent is expected to choose 36. The 36 choices he or she makes constitute, in effect, a limited, incomplete but (we think) useful profile of his or her religious imagination. The four profiles charted through each of the small matrices or the one large profile charted through all the matrices are, for the purposes of this book, a measure of the religious imagination of each of the 2,500 young adults (in the United States and Canada) to whom questionnaires were administered. In Figure 2.1 (page 26) we have charted the "average" profile for men and women in the United States. The lines indicate how the "typical" young American Catholic—man or woman—imagine Jesus and Mary, God and heaven. The pertinent question in the present book is whether these profile lines are useful for understanding the religious attitudes and behavior of young Americans.

The mean scores in Table 2.1 (page 26) and the profile lines in Figure 2.1 (page 25) show positive images of both Jesus and Mary, somewhat stronger for women than for men, but strong for both groups. The most popular adjectival descriptions of Jesus and Mary are "gentle," "warm," "patient," and "comforting"; the least popular for Mary are "stern," "distant," "demanding," "irrelevant," and "challenging." Jesus is considerably more likely to be thought of by both men and women as stern than is Mary, and somewhat more likely to be thought of, at least by men, as distant and demanding. Nevertheless, for young Catholic adults the profile of their imagined pictures, their "stories" of Jesus and Mary, tend to be warm and positive. Indeed, in the case of Mary it is strikingly positive, considering the low level of emphasis the Church has placed on devotion to Mary since the Vatican Council.

The most popular pictures of life after death for young adults is heaven as a life of peace and tranquility, a spiritual life involving mind but not body, and a place of loving, intellectual communion with God and reunion with loved ones. However, some young Catholics are not prepared to exclude the possibility that heaven includes things that make our life here on earth pleasurable.

FIGURE 2.1

A. Of course, no one knows exactly what life after death would be like, but here are some ideas people have had. How likely do you feel each possibility is?

(Circle One Number Beside Each Idea)

	Very likely	Somewhat likely	Not too likely	Not likely at all
1. A life of peace and tranquility	1	2	3	4
2. A life of intense action	1	2	3	4
3. A life like the one here on earth only better	1	2	3	4
4. A life without many things which make our present life enjoyable	1	2	3	4
5. A pale shadowy form of life, hardly life at all	1	2	3	4
6. A spiritual life, involving our mind but not our body	1	2	3	4
7. A paradise of pleasure and delights	1	2	3	4
8. A place of loving intellectual communion	1	2	3	4
9. Union with God	1	2	3	4
10. Reunion with loved ones	1	2	3	4

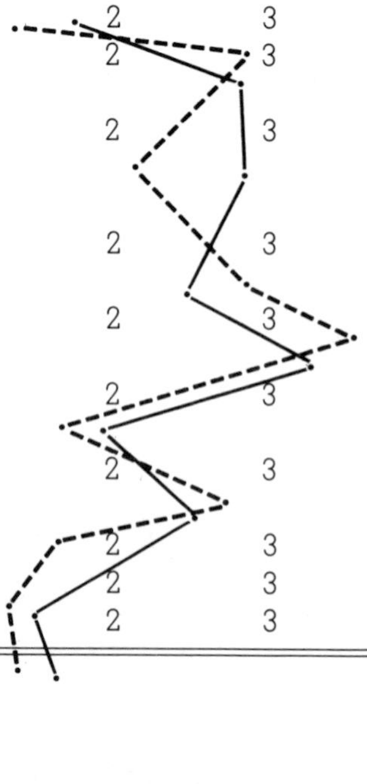

B. When you think about God, how likely are each of these images to come to your mind?

(Circle One Number For Each Word)

	Extremely likely	Somewhat likely	Not too likely	Not likely at all
Judge	1	2	3	4
Protector	1	2	3	4
Redeemer	1	2	3	4
Lover	1	2	3	4
Master	1	2	3	4
Mother	1	2	3	4
Creator	1	2	3	4
Father	1	2	3	4

C. Here are some words people sometimes associate with Jesus. How likely is each one of them to come to your mind when you think about Jesus?

(Circle One Number For Each Word)

	Extremely likely	Somewhat likely	Not too likely	Not likely at all
Gentle	1	2	3	4
Stern	1	2	3	4
Warm	1	2	3	4
Distant	1	2	3	4
Demanding	1	2	3	4
Patient	1	2	3	4
Irrelevant	1	2	3	4
Challenging	1	2	3	4
Comforting	1	2	3	4

D. Now think about Jesus' mother, Mary. How likely is each word to come to your mind when you think of Mary?

(Circle One Number For Each Word)

	Extremely likely	Somewhat likely	Not too likely	Not likely at all
Gentle	1	2	3	4
Stern	1	2	3	4
Warm	1	2	3	4
Distant	1	2	3	4
Demanding	1	2	3	4
Patient	1	2	3	4
Irrelevant	1	2	3	4
Challenging	1	2	3	4
Comforting	1	2	3	4

——— Men
— — — Women

TABLE 2.1

Mean Values for Items Comprising Measures of
Religious Imagination for Men and Women

MEN		WOMEN	
Mean	Label	Mean	Label
2.209	Image of God as Judge	2.345	Image of God as Judge
1.795	Image of God as Protector	1.478	Image of God as Protector
1.970	Image of God as Redeemer	1.280	Image of God as Redeemer
2.448	Image of God as Lover	2.599	Image of God as Lover
2.069	Image of God as Master	1.994	Image of God as Master
3.124	Image of God as Mother	2.968	Image of God as Mother
1.411	Image of God as Creator	1.301	Image of God as Creator
1.699	Image of God as Father	1.556	Image of God as Father
1.476	Jesus as Gentle	1.287	Jesus as Gentle
2.365	Jesus as Stern	2.535	Jesus as Stern
1.493	Jesus as Warm	1.271	Jesus as Warm
2.933	Jesus as Distant	3.000	Jesus as Distant
2.731	Jesus as Demanding	2.962	Jesus as Demanding
1.479	Jesus as Patient	1.276	Jesus as Patient
3.362	Jesus as Irrelevant	3.404	Jesus as Irrelevant
2.510	Jesus as Challenging	2.504	Jesus as Challenging
1.566	Jesus as Comforting	1.298	Jesus as Comforting
1.291	Mary as Gentle	1.157	Mary as Gentle
3.003	Mary as Stern	3.092	Mary as Stern
1.362	Mary as Warm	1.188	Mary as Warm
3.053	Mary as Distant	3.122	Mary as Distant
3.192	Mary as Demanding	3.328	Mary as Demanding
1.468	Mary as Patient	1.247	Mary as Patient
3.274	Mary as Irrelevant	3.390	Mary as Irrelevant
3.063	Mary as Challenging	3.086	Mary as Challenging
1.468	Mary as Comforting	1.239	Mary as Comforting
1.633	Peace and Tranquility After Death	1.499	Peace and Tranquility After Death
2.846	Intense Action After Death	2.919	Intense Action After Death
2.328	Similar Life After Death	2.288	Similar Life After Death
2.654	Lack Things After Death	2.740	Lack Things After Death
3.239	Shadow Life After Death	3.288	Shadow Life After Death
2.017	Spirit Life After Death	1.938	Spirit Life After Death
2.331	Paradise After Death	2.328	Paradise After Death
2.036	Intellectual Communion After Death	1.842	Intellectual Communion After Death
1.579	Union With God After Death	1.363	Union With God After Death
1.722	Reunion After Death	1.470	Reunion After Death

The images of God as "protector," "master," "creator," "father," and "redeemer" are more attractive for young Catholics than the picture of God as lover. The picture of God as mother received the lowest of all the mean scores (though one quarter of the young Catholic adults say they are somewhat likely to think of God as a mother).

God is less attractive than either Jesus or Mary. Rather more harsh images, such as "judge" and "master," seem to have a stronger impact on the imagination of young Catholics than the image of "lover." Indeed, for both young men and women, the tender and gentle imagery of God as lover and mother seems to be the picture often found in their religious imaginations.

It is altogether possible that the different wording of the questions for Jesus and Mary on the one hand and for God on the other explain the apparent greater attractiveness of Jesus and Mary in preference to the heavenly faith it was their mission to reveal. But it is more likely that emphasis on the power, majesty, and righteousness of God has made him a much more distant and less attractive figure for young Catholics than are Jesus and Mary, who have human faces like ours and engage in human behavior something like ours. (As we will note subsequently, the religious imagination of Protestants contains an even more distant and less attractive picture of God.)

A statistical technique called factor analysis was used to reduce the profiles in Figure 2.1 and Table 2.1 to a number of scales which measured response patterns to religious imagination questions among our respondents. The principal factors for Jesus and Mary were ones that emphasized, on the one hand, the gentle, warm, patient, comforting picture of these personages and, on the other, the stern, distant, demanding, irrelevant, and challenging pictures. There were three different response patterns in the imagination of the afterlife: 1) a "union" pattern, stressing the last three items—a place of loving intellectual communion, union with God and reunion with loved ones, life of peace and tranquility; 2) a factor which stressed the vagueness of the hereafter—a life without anything which makes our present life enjoyable, a place, shadowy form of life, hardly life at all, and a spiritual life involving our mind and not our body; 3) the third factor presented a much more dynamic vision of heaven—a life of intense action, a paradise of pleasure and delights, life like one here on earth only better (a factor which, by the way, does represent thoroughly orthodox Christianity, at least as I understand it). There were two God factors, one stressing the judge, protector, redeemer, master, creator, and father pictures; and the other stressing God as lover and mother. These nine factors, then, represent nine short profiles of the religious imagination of young Catholics. For analytic purposes of the present, four of the nine factors were selected because, in addition to representing the more positive and more "gracious" story of God, they also discriminated more effectively among different kinds of religious and social attitudes and behaviors. The four scales were the Jesus and Mary as "warm," God as "mother/lover" scale, and heaven as a "paradise and action-filled life like our own" scale.

In Table 2.2 one can observe the differences between young men and young women on these four scales. Young women are somewhat more likely to think of God as a mother and lover and of Jesus and Mary as warm than are their male counterparts, though there is little difference between the two in their estimates of heaven as a life of paradise and action.

TABLE 2.2

"Stories of God" by Sex
(Percent high)

	Men	Women
God as mother and lover	31	36
Heaven as paradise of pleasure and action	29	21
Jesus as "warm"[a]	40	59
Mary as "warm"[a]	56	72

[a] Proportion checking all of the following as "extremely likely," "warm," "patient," "gentle," "comforting."

By yet further factor analysis, we reduced the four scales to two (Table 2.3, page 29), and then, finally one "principal component" scale. These three factors—the God/heaven, the Jesus/Mary, and the "grace" factor, the last combining the first two—are the principal measures of the religious imagination which will be used in this book. Note in Table 2.3 that women are much higher than men in the proportions who check all four favorable adjectives of both Jesus and Mary. Hence, they are somewhat higher on the composite "grace" scale than are men.

Ordinarily, in the analysis to be presented in this book, we will use the "grace" scale as a dependent variable because it is the single, doubtless oversimplified, measure of the religious imagination and also one which discriminates sharply among population groups and powerfully predicts attitudes and behaviors. However, in the course of the analysis being summarized in this volume, we also tested the other scales. When one of them makes a special or important contribution to our understanding of the impact of the religious imagination (e.g., the influence of God as mother and lover scale on sexual permissiveness), it will be discussed.

TABLE 2.3

"Stories of God" by Sex

(Percent High)

	Men	Women
God/heaven [a]	25	25
Jesus/Mary [b]	32	53
"Grace" [c]	20	29

[a] The God/heaven scale is a factor made up of God as mother and lover and heaven a life of intense action, a life like the present only better, and a paradise of pleasure and delight.
[b] Jesus/Mary scale proportion checking all 8 responses as "extremely" likely.
[c] "Grace" scale factor combining God, Heaven, Jesus, and Mary scales.

The summary measure is named the "grace" scale, not for theological reasons but for reasons of sociological theory; for the scale combines measures which indicate a very warm, positive, gracious view of the story of the relationship between God and the individual human person—warmth, gentleness, comfort, patience, tender, maternal love, and a future of action and pleasure which improves upon but does not negate our present life. It is a "story of God" which is benign and attractive. The two principal questions to be asked in the present book are: What life experiences incline one to have such a story of God? What effect does such a story have on human attitudes and behaviors?

Experience, Imagination and Devotion

Highlights

1 *Religious experiences strongly affect the religious imagination and correlate both positively and strongly with stories of God, heaven, Jesus, Mary, and grace (Tables 3.3, 3.4).*

2 *The religious imagination relates to whether one has thought about a religious vocation, and whether one is able to respond hopefully to a tragic situation (Table 3.8).*

3 *The religious picture and the religious experience are much more likely to produce desirable religious attitudes and behaviors than are doctrinal propositions (Table 3.10).*

4 *A tender, loving story of God, heaven, Jesus and Mary correlates negatively with "radical" sexual attitudes, but there is no significant correlation between the same kind of religious imagination and "liberal" sexual attitudes (Table 3.12).*

5 *A Church concerned about its credibility and effectiveness in the contemporary world, while not abandoning doctrinal orthodoxy, must rediscover the importance of the religious imagination.*

Chapter 3

Experience, Imagination, and Devotion

This chapter will test two of our theoretical expectations:
- That religious experience and sensitivity to nature will have a positive effect on a person's religious story.
- That the religious story in turn will have a positive effect on religious devotion, as measured by a number of different indicators, and, indeed, a much stronger effect than would propositional religion as measures by a scale of doctrinal orthodoxy.

A fundamental problem that will affect much of the analysis in this book must be made clear at the beginning. Let us suppose that a religious sensitivity to nature correlates with the grace scale: those that are more religiously sensitive to nature will have a more benign and gracious story of God in their religious imagination. Might not the causal flow move the other way around? Might not those high on the grace scale be more sensitive to nature precisely because they have a more benign story of the meaning of their lives? How can one be sure that "nature" affects "grace" instead of the other way around?

Virtually every relationship to be discussed in this book may flow in the opposite direction than hypothesized in the flow chart in Chapter 1. In some cases a strongly persuasive argument can be made about the direction of the flow.

Granting that questions of causality are difficult to sort out, there are several reasons for using the model in Figure 1.1 as a starting point—until longitudinal research on the same respondents makes possible more confident answers about the development of the religious imagination.

1. The theory hypothesizes a relationship between sensitivity to nature and a "grace-full" story of God. This chapter does indeed sustain that hypothesis. No one has suggested the opposite hypothesis, that those with a graceful story of God are more likely to be religiously influenced by nature because it is a hypothesis that has inherently somewhat less probability.

2. The relationship between a benign story of God and sensitivity to nature is an important finding and one with not inconsiderable implication for both theology and policy regardless of the direction of the casual flow.

3. In a real world both variables are likely to influence one another. A religious sensitivity to nature is likely to lead to and enhance imagination and graciousness, while a gracious story of the meaning of the cosmos and of human life is very likely to render a person more sensitive to the religious implications of nature.

In our research of young Catholic adults we asked three different questions about religious experience:
1. "How often in your life have you had an experience where you felt you were very close to a powerful spiritual force that seemed to lift you out of yourself?"
2. "Have you ever had the experience of knowing confidently that your life has a purpose which goes beyond the limitations of your present existence?"
3. "Have you ever felt that you were in direct contact with the sacred or the holy?"

Half of our young adults (Table 3.1, page 35) report the powerful spiritual force experience, a little more than half the purpose in life experience, and 40 percent contact with the sacred experience. If one combines these three experiences in one scale (Table 3.2, page 35), some 30 percent of the young adults say they have had none of these experiences, while 20 percent have had at least one of the experiences frequently. The rest of the sample lie somewhere in between frequent experiences and no experiences at all. (As we progress in our research on religious experiences, we hope to develop more measures to adequately tap the various kinds of encounters with "otherness.")

Furthermore, about one third of our young adults (Table 3.3, page 35) report that they learned "a great deal" about the meaning of life from nature. ("Here are some ways of learning about life and the forces governing them. Please indicate how much you think you can learn about life from . . . getting close to nature.") Do the various religious experiences, as summarized in the "combined religious experience scale," affect one's religious imagination? Table 3.4 (page 36) suggests that they do strongly. Those who are high on the spiritual experience scale are more than three times as likely as those who had no religious experience to think of God as a lover and a mother and heaven as an action-filled paradise. They are more than twice as likely to be in the top quartile on the grace scale as those who have had no religious experience and 14 percentage points more likely to use all eight of the "warm" adjectives in their description of Jesus and Mary. As I hypothesized, then, religious experiences do indeed correlate both positively and strongly with stories of God, heaven, Jesus, Mary, and grace.

TABLE 3.1

Religious Experiences Among Young American Catholics
(Percent)

	Powerful Spiritual Force	Purpose in Life	Contact With
Never	49	44	61
Once or twice	29	24	22
Several times	16	17	9
Frequently	5	16	8
Total	100	100	100

TABLE 3.2

Combined Spiritual Experience Scale
(Percent)

None	30
Almost none	16
A few	18
Several	23
Many	19
Total	100

TABLE 3.3

Learning About Life From Nature
(Percent)

A great deal	32
Some	42
Little	21
None	5

Similarly (Table 3.5, page 36), those who have learned a great deal about the meaning of life from nature are four times as likely to be in the upper quartile in the grace scale, twice as likely to be high on the God/heaven scale (22 percent versus 10 percent), and also almost twice as likely (49 percent versus 27 percent) to use all the "warm" adjectives of Jesus and Mary. Both religious experiences and learning about the meaning of life from nature correlate strongly and positively with gracious stories of God. The religious imagination is profoundly affected by the religious experience and by sensitivity to nature.

TABLE 3.4

Religious Story Scales by Religious Experience
(Percent High)

	"Grace" Scale	God/Heaven Scale	Jesus/Mary Scale
None	14	11	35
Almost None	16	15	41
A few	24	24	44
Several	24	26	47
Many	34	36	49

TABLE 3.5

Religious Story Scales by Nature as a Source of Life Meaning
(Percent)

	"Grace" Scale	God/Heaven Scale	Jesus/Mary Scale
A great deal	37	22	49
Some	21	22	46
Little	16	19	33
Nothing	9	10	27

These relationships are summarized in correlational statistics in Table 3.6 (page 37). Religious experience relates at approximately a .2 level with the grace scale and with its two principal components, the God/heaven and the Jesus/Mary scales; and there is a .16 relationship between a "gracious" story of God or, if one wishes, a gracious religious imagination, and sensitivity to nature as a source of life meaning.

The first hypotheses expressed in the flow chart in Chapter 1 (Figure 1.1, page 20) are sustained. There are significant correlations between religious experience and sensitivity to nature on the one hand and the religious imagination on the other.

It is possible to explore the flow of causality between religious experience and grace story by asking respondents what effect, if any, the religious experience had on them and see whether those effects do indeed correlate with the grace story. If they do, it is at least highly probable that some of the causal flow is from the experience to the story instead of vice versa. We did ask those respondents who had the experience of being in the presence of a powerful spiritual force that seemed to lift you out of yourself how the experience affected their lives.

TABLE 3.6

Correlations Between
Experiences and Religious Stories
(Coefficient of Correlation = Pearson's r)

	"Grace" Scale	God/Heaven Scale	Jesus/Mary Scale
Religious Experience	.21	.22	.19
Nature a source of life meaning	.16	.09	.15

Survey Questions

How did this experience affect your life?

(Circle as many as apply)

Not at all 01
I became more prayerful 02
I became a better person 03
I was more considerate of others 04
I began to think of a Church vocation 05
I knew everything would be all right 06
Other (Please describe below) 07

Only 13 percent reported no effects at all, and each of the other effects did correlate positively with the grace story. Thus if one creates a scale of the sort in Table 3.6, one can see that those who report two or more effects on their life of the religious experience (the three effects considered were more prayerful, a better person, and more confident things would be all right) are twice as likely to be in the upper quartile of the grace scale as those who have had no religious experience, and 14 percentage points higher than those who report the experience had no effect on them. This argument does not prove there is no flow of causality from stories to experience. It does seem to establish that there is some flow from experience to story, which is the only assumption being made in this chapter, as well as in this book.

What good is the religious imagination? What influence does it have on religious behavior? What relationship can be found between gracious and tender stories of God and other measures of religiousness? Just as the religious imagination is strongly correlated with both religious experience and sensitivity to nature, so also it strongly relates to several different measures of religious attitudes and behaviors. Those who are high on the religious imagination scale (Table 3.7) are more likely to go to Mass every week, to receive communion every week, and to pray every day. Indeed, the ones who are high on the grace scale are either twice as likely or almost twice as likely in comparison with those who are low on the scale to be weekly churchgoers, weekly communicants, and daily prayers. The religious imagination has a very powerful impact on religious devotion.

TABLE 3.7

Religious Devotion by "Grace" Story
(Percent)

	Weekly Mass	Weekly Communion	Daily Prayer
Grace Scale	26	14	19
(low	35	20	37
to	35	21	36
high)	42	31	47

The religious imagination (Table 3.8, page 41) also relates to whether one has thought about religious vocation, and whether one is able to respond hopefully to a description of a tragic situation.

Survey Questions

Which of the following *best* expresses your attitude toward a religious vocation?

I am presently a priest, brother, or nun . . . .
01 - Skip to 81
I am presently training for the religious life . . . .
02 - Skip to 81
I am seriously considering a religious vocation but have not begun training . . . .
03 - Skip to 81
I have trained for a religious vocation or have actually taken vows but later decided that the religious life is not for me . . . .
04 - Answer 80A & B
I have seriously considered a religious vocation but decided against it before entering a seminary or convent . . . .
05 - Answer 80A & B

The thought of becoming a priest, brother, or nun has entered my mind but I have never really seriously considered it ....

06 - Answer 80A & B

I have never considered a religious vocation ....

07 - Answer 80A & B

Here is a situation in which some people actually find themselves. Imagine that this is happening to you. How close would each of the following statements be to your own reaction to such a situation?

You have just visited your doctor and he has told you that you have less than a year to live. He has said that your disease is incurable.

Please circle a number on each line to indicate if the statement comes *very close* to your feelings, *not at all close* to your feelings, or is *somewhere in between* these feelings.

	Very close . . . . Not at all close
A. It will all work out for the best somehow	1 . . . 2 . . . 3 . . . 4 . . . 5
B. No one should question the good-ness of God's decision about death	1 . . . 2 . . . 3 . . . 4 . . . 5
C. There is nothing to do but wait for the end	1 . . . 2 . . . 3 . . . 4 . . . 5
D. I am angry and depressed at the unfairness of it all	1 . . . 2 . . . 3 . . . 4 . . . 5
E. I am thankful for the life that I have had	1 . . . 2 . . . 3 . . . 4 . . . 5
F. I cannot explain why this has happened to me, but I still believe in God's love	1 . . . 2 . . . 3 . . . 4 . . . 5

Here is another situation in which some people actually find themselves. Imagine that one of your parents is dying a slow and painful death. How close would each of the following statements be to your own reaction to such a situation?

Please circle a number on each line to indicate if the statement comes *very close* to your feelings, *not at all close* to your feelings, or is *somewhere in between* these feelings.

	Very close	Not at all close
A. They are in pain now, but they will be at peace soon	1 ... 2 ... 3 ... 4 ... 5	
B. Everything that happens is God's will and cannot be bad	1 ... 2 ... 3 ... 4 ... 5	
C. There is nothing to do but wait for the end	1 ... 2 ... 3 ... 4 ... 5	
D. This waiting is inhuman for them; I hope it will end soon	1 ... 2 ... 3 ... 4 ... 5	
E. We can at least be thankful for the good life we have had together	1 ... 2 ... 3 ... 4 ... 5	
F. This is tragic, but death is not the ultimate end for us	1 ... 2 ... 3 ... 4 ... 5	

The hopeful response is contained in Item F of each of the two questions. Forty-two percent of those who were high on the "grace" scale (the top quartile) were likely to have thought of a vocation, 13 percent have thought of it seriously, and 42 percent respond hopefully to tragic situations (as opposed to 15 percent of those who were low on the scale). On the matter of religious vocations there can be little doubt about the flow of causality. No one would seriously contend that because a young person thinks about a religious vocation seriously, this thought would improve the graciousness of his religious imagination.

Mass, communion, prayer, vocational attitude, and response to tragedy are all connected with the pictures and images one has of God, Jesus, Mary, and the afterlife. In Table 3.9 (page 41) one can examine the relationship between these five measures of religious imagination and (a) the grace scale, (b) religious experience, and

(c) doctrinal orthodoxy. Note that the doctrinal orthodoxy scale used is constructed of the following items:

1. "Jesus directly handed over the leadership of his Church to Peter and the popes";

2. "It is a sin for a Catholic to miss weekly Mass obligation when he easily could have attended";

3. "Under certain conditions the pope is infallible (cannot be wrong) when he speaks of matters of faith and morals."

TABLE 3.8

Religious Attitudes by "Grace" Story
(Percent)

	Thought of Vocation	Thought Seriously of Vocation	Hopeful Response to Tragedy
(low	26	1	15
to	35	6	23
high)	35	7	31
	42	13	43

It is obvious that the pictures in the religious imagination and the experience of the sacred, or of hopefulness, or of overwhelming spiritual power are far more powerfully related to Mass, communion, prayer, vocation, and hopefulness than is doctrinal orthodoxy. The religious picture and the religious experience, in other words, are much more likely to produce desirable religious attitudes and behaviors than are the appropriate and proper doctrinal propositions.

TABLE 3.9

Correlations Between Religious Story, Orthodoxy and Devotion
(Coefficient of Correlation = Pearson's r)

	Mass	Communion	Prayer	Vocation	Hopefulness
Grace	.18	.15	.25	.13	.34
Orthodoxy	.07	.02	.08	.07	.11
Experience	.09	.13	.24	.30	.31

Correlations not statistically significant.

The correlations in Table 3.9 are "r's," that is to say, the simple raw correlation between, for example, grace and prayer. Such a relationship does not take into account the possibility that grace,

41

othodoxy, and experience may also relate to one another. If one should separate out the influence that is attributable solely let us say, to grace *net* of orthodoxy and experience, the correlation will diminish somewhat or substantially. A mathematical process called "multiple regression" enables one to obtain the net relationship between two variables and eliminate the influence of the other variables that are entered into the equation. The "standardized" or "net" correlation is called "beta." We will use these raw and standardized measures repeatedly in subsequent chapters. The professional social scientist understands immediately what they are; the non-social scientist need merely note that the beta is a measure of a more "pure" relationship between two variables.

A quick inspection of Table 3.10 illustrates the following:
1. The relationship between the religious imagination and religious devotion is only minimally affected by standardization techniques, save for the relation between the religious imagination and the thought about religious vocation.
2. Doctrinal orthodoxy does not have a statistically significant relation with four of the five measures of religious devotion that we are considering. (It only correlates significantly with the hopeful response to tragedy, and even here it is a much less powerful influence than either grace or religious experience.)
3. While generally not as powerful a predictor of devotion as the religious imagination (save in the case of serious thought about a vocation), religious experience nonetheless does relate significantly to all the measures of religious devotion save weekly Mass attendance. At least some of the impact, then, of religious experience on religious devotion is mediated through the fact that religious imagination makes a "gracious" religious story more likely, and such a story in its turn makes religious devotion more likely.

TABLE 3.10

Standardized Correlations for Religious Story, Orthodoxy and Devotion
(Betas)

	Mass	Communion	Prayer	Vocation	Hopefulness
Grace	.18	.18	.21	.06	.29
Orthodox	.03*	.03*	.05*	.05*	.09
Experience	.03*	.09	.19	.28	.23

* Correlation not statistically significant.

Religious imagination is much more likely to lead to Mass
attendance, communion reception, serious thought about a

religious vocation, and a hopeful response to tragedy than is propositional orthodoxy. If religious leaders wish to improve levels of religious devotion, the obvious strategy is not to reassert propositional orthodoxy but to promote more "gracious" stories of God.

A "gracious" religious imagination is also likely to inhibit departures from the Catholic Church (Table 3.11). Those who are on the lower half of the grace scale are half again as likely to have left behind their Catholic origins as those who are high on the grace scale. Not only does a religious imagination containing warm images of Jesus and Mary, loving and tender images of God, and pleasurable, action-filled images of the hereafter incline a young person to be more devout, it also inclines him/her to be substantially more likely to stay within the boundaries of Catholicism.

TABLE 3.11

Leaving the Church and "Grace" Story
(Percent Leaving)

(low	16
	16
to	
	12
high)	10

If one is "indulgent" in one's religious imagination and permits in it soft, warm, tender, loving, affectionate, pleasurable images, is not one likely to be more permissive sexually?

The exact opposite seems to be the case (Table 3.12, page 44). Those who are high on the grace scale are *less* likely to be permissive in their attitudes about living together, abortion when there is a chance of a defective infant or when the woman wants no more children, divorce, birth control, and homosexuality. The only item in Table 3.12 in which there is no relationship between grace and sexual attitudes is the one that asks young people whether they think updating the Church's sexual ethics on birth control and divorce is a matter of considerable importance for the Church.

It ought to be noted that while there is indeed a negative correlation between the grace scale and permissiveness, even those who are high on the grace scale are scarcely likely to endorse in overwhelming numbers of orthodox sexual position. Two fifths of those who are on the upper quartile of the grace scale do not think that living together before marriage is wrong. Only one-quarter think that abortion is wrong if there is a risk of a defective child; only 17 percent think that divorce is wrong; and only 10 percent think that birth control is wrong. The people who are high on the grace scale, in other words, may well be permissive by the absolute standards of official Catholic doctrine, but they are notably less permissive than those who are low on the grace scale.

TABLE 3.12

Sexual Attitudes by "Grace" Story
(Percent)

	Living together (Always Wrong)	Abortion— Defective Child (Wrong)	Abortion— Wants no more Children (Right)	Divorce (Wrong)	Birth Control (Wrong)	Homosex- uality (Wrong)	Updating sex- ual ethics important
(low	43	14	29	10	4	57	48
to	48	15	34	11	4	66	53
high)	59	16	50	11	7	65	57
	60	27	51	17	10	74	49

The seven sexual items, blended into a factor analysis, produced two different dimensions of sexual attitudes, a "radical" and a "liberal" factor. The first loads heavily on abortion if the woman wants no children, homosexuality, and living together before marriage; the second loads heavily on birth control, abortion when there is the possibility of a defective child, divorce, and the need for sexual updating by the Church. A tender, loving story of God, heaven, Jesus, and Mary correlates *negatively* with "radical" sexual attitudes, but there is no significant correlation between the same kind of religious imagination and "liberal" sexual attitudes. However, in neither case does a loving, affectionate, graceful religious imagination correlate significantly and positively with permissiveness. If your religious imagination is graceful, you are more likely to be against "radical" sexual permissiveness and to be little different from other Catholics on matters like birth control and divorce—though surely no more sympathetic to unorthodox sexual positions than other Catholics. A warm religious imagination, then, does not produce sexual permissiveness, but seems to be the Church's strongest asset in resisting sexual permissiveness. Those whose religious imagination involves them in an intense love relationship with God are more likely to be cautious and careful—and "traditional" in their human love relationships.

To confirm this perhaps counterintuitive finding, let us take a look at an item which some critics have termed an "Islamic" view of heaven as a paradise of pleasure and delight. If you think God is preparing for you a sensual paradise, are you not more likely to seek out such delights, even when they are illicit in this life? And if you think of God as a passionate lover, are you not more likely to find some justification for promiscuous relationships in anticipation of that divine passion?

TABLE 3.13

Correlations Between Grace Story and Two Sex Scales
(Coefficient of Correlation = Pearson's r)

	"Radical"[a] Sex	"Liberal"[b] Sex
Grace	−.22	.02*

[a] Abortion, no more children, living together, homosexuality
[b] Birth control, divorce, abortion defective child, and sexual updating
* Correlation not statistically significant.

Table 3.14 confirms for the specific item the picture we have already described. The lowest approval rating for living together before marriage can be found precisely among those who think of God as a lover and who think of heaven as a paradise of pleasure and delight. "Sensual" religious imagery negatively correlates with sexual permissiveness—a point which may shock some religious leaders who would have expected the opposite. Some people will doubtless continue to expect it despite contrary evidence.

TABLE 3.14

Living Together by God as Lover and Heaven as a Pleasure of Paradise and Delights
(Percent living together before marriage is never wrong)

	God a Lover	Heaven a Paradise of pleasure & delights
Extremely likely	39	36
Somewhat likely	55	51
Not too likely	58	57
Not at all likely	62	59

Finally, those with a graceful religious imagination are more likely to be grateful (Tables 3.15, 3.16, page 46). Two thirds of those who are high on the grace scale say that they often offer prayers of thanksgiving, as opposed to 44 percent of those who are low on that scale. (Would anyone seriously suggest that the prayers of thanksgiving influence the religious imagination instead of the other way around?) And, while both the grace scale and religious experience correlate positively and significantly with prayers of gratitude, religious orthodoxy does not relate significantly with such prayers. Believing that the pope is the infallible successor to Peter, in other words, does not incline young Catholics either to greater devotion or greater gratitude. But gracious religious images do indeed make young Catholics able to respond gratefully to the origin and the source of giftedness.

TABLE 3.15

Grace Scale and Prayers of Gratitude
(Percent often say prayers of thanksgiving)

"Grace"	44
(low	52
to	56
high)	68

TABLE 3.16

Correlations Between "Grace" Scale and Prayers of Gratitude

	r	beta
"Grace"	.19	.13
Orthodoxy	.09	.06*
Religious experience	.19	.14

* Correlation not significant.

The "so what?" of the religious imagination has been as powerfully established in this chapter as social science evidence is likely to be able to establish it. The pictures or images of God, heaven, Jesus, and Mary have a profound effect on other aspects of people's religious behavior. (As Brother Thomas Hoffman will demonstrate later, they also have a powerful effect on social action involvement and concerns.) Shaped in part by religious experiences and by religious sensitivity to nature, the pictures and stories in the religious imagination are far more important than doctrinal orthodoxy in affecting what young Catholics do and what they believe religiously.

TABLE 3.17

Relationship Between Grace Scale and
Perceived Effect of Religious Experience[a]

(Percent in Upper Quartile)

No experience	17
	N = (998)
No perceived effect	20
	N = (195)
One perceived effect	28
	N = (236)
Two or more effects	34
	N = (134)

[a] The experience of being in the presence of an overwhelming spiritual force which seems to lift you out of yourself.

It is not my intention to deny the importance of doctrinal orthodoxy, much less to suggest that the Church abandon its concern about orthodoxy. My point is that if orthodoxy is important, religious imagination is more important—a fact which has rarely been doubted over most of the years of Church history. Even when debates about orthodoxy were carried on by theologians, bishops, kings, and emperors, the religious tradition was passed on to ordinary people by means of pictures, images, and stories, by stained glass windows and liturgies, and by miracle and morality plays. The evidence presented in this chapter suggests that such is still the case. While we may not have stained glass windows and morality plays, the pictures in the religious imagination are still more important in affecting religous behavior than doctrinal propositions. A Church concerned about its credibility and effectiveness in the contemporary world should not abandon its defense of doctrinal orthodoxy; but it also would be well advised to rediscover the importance of the religious imagination, especially if one concedes to Church leaders the fact that there is a "neopagan" sexual morality at work in the world. The single most effective counterforce to that pagan sexual ethic is a religious imagination which emphasizes God's warmth, tender love, and pleasurable rewards.

The Family of Origin

Highlights

1   *The principal "sacrament" by which loving goodness is revealed to us are other human beings. Family relationships have a powerful influence on religious imagination.*

2   *There are three different patterns of relationships in the family triad: one for Jesus, one for Mary, and one for God. For young men what is really important in enhancing all three of their images is to be close to both parents. For young women, to enhance their stories of Jesus and Mary, it is necessary for them to be close to their fathers.*

3   *A joyous approach to religion by both parents affects whether there is joy in the religious imagination of children (Table 4.7).*

4   *There is no negative impact on the grace story by the mother pursuing a career or holding a job. In fact, there is some reason to believe that a working mother may enhance a young woman's story of grace (Table 4.8).*

5   *Closeness to both parents for a son, closeness to a father for a daughter, and a closeness of parents to one another for children of both sexes are necessary for a young person to receive an image of loving goodness.*

6   *The exercise of authority in the family seems to make little difference in the religious imagination of either son or daughter (Table 4.10). The religious devotion of parents affects the religious imagination of children. Men are almost completely unaffected by their father's communion and strongly affected by their mother's. Women seem to be affected by both parents (Tables 4.11, 4.12).*

Chapter 4

The Family of Origin

Our life story is a story of human relationships. So it is reasonable to expect that our religious story will be heavily influenced by human relationships. Nature plays a role in the development of the religious imagination, as do "direct" experiences of God. However, the principal "sacraments" by which loving goodness is revealed to us are other human beings. It is logical to assume that the family in which we grow up (the "family of origin"), the relationships we have with members of the family as well as relationships they have with one another, will have a powerful influence on our religious imagination.

TABLE 4.1

Family Structure in Which
Catholic Young Adults Grew Up
(Percent)

Very close to both parents	14
Both parents joyous religiously	23
Parents related very well	35
Mother influenced religious life very much	33
Father influenced religious life very much	22

The first question to be asked is whether the relationships a child has with his or her parents affects the religious imagination. Our respondents were asked about their relationship with both their mother and their father. A joint scale was composed (Tables 4.1, 4.2, 4.3, page 52), ranking the young adults as to whether they were close to both parents, with their mother but not their father, father but not to mother, or close to neither. The most powerful impact on the grace scale came when the young person reported that he or she was very close to both parents. This group was three times as likely to be in the upper quartile of the grace scale as those who said they were close to neither parent. For young men there was some increment to the scale if they were close to one parent or the other, but it did not matter which parent. Young women who were close to at least one parent were twice as likely to be in the top quartile, with the greater impact coming from closeness to the father. Closeness to one parent is better than closeness to neither parent, especially for young women, and for them more especially if they are close to their father.

TABLE 4.1A

Grace Scale by Closeness to Parents by Sex
(Percent in upper quartile)

	Men	Women
Very close to neither	16	12
Very close to mother	19	25
Very close to father	20	29
Very close to both	38	37

TABLE 4.2

"God/Heaven" Scale by Closeness to Parents by Sex
(Percent high)

	Men	Women
Very close to neither	21	25
Very close to mother	29	23
Very close to father	29	25
Very close to both	32	28

TABLE 4.3

Jesus/Mary Scale by Closeness to Parents by Sex
(Percent high)

	Men	Women
Very close to neither	28	56
Very close to mother	34	53
Very close to father	36	59
Very close to both	41	65

For young men, closeness to both parents has an especially powerful effect on the God-heaven scale. A story of God as mother and lover and heaven as a paradise of pleasure and delight seems to have little impact on the young women's responses (Table 4.2).

Among men, images of Jesus and Mary are also strikingly affected by their experience of closeness to their parents, with the father having more of an impact than the mother. For young women, however, the important experience that affects the Jesus/Mary story is the experience of being close to both parents.

Variations in the effect of closeness to parents for young men and young women suggest a complex dynamic in the family triad with the sex of parent and child both being important (Tables 4.4—4.6). For young men, closeness to one parent is enough to raise their score on the Mary scale, while for young women, higher on the scale to begin with, a notable increase comes if they are close to their father or to both parents. The vision of Mary as reflecting the womanliness of God, in other words, is enhanced for boys by being close to either parent, but for girls it is enhanced by being close to the father, and even more if they are close to both parents.

TABLE 4.4

Mary Scale by Closeness to Parents by Sex
(Percent all four adjectives)

	Men	Women
Very close to neither	53	69
Very close to mother	62	73
Very close to father	63	77
Very close to both	69	82

TABLE 4.5

Jesus Scale by Closeness to Parents by Sex
(Percent all four adjectives)

	Men	Women
Very close to neither	37	57
Very close to mother	37	58
Very close to father	41	65
Very close to both	52	70

The same effect exists for a young woman as far as her image of Jesus is concerned. Closeness to mother does not notably enhance the image of Jesus, but closeness to father does. There is some additional increment for the young woman if she is close to both parents. The young men, however, show a notable effect on the Jesus image only if they are close to both parents. Young men need closeness to one parent to enhance their image of Mary, closeness to both parents to enhance their image of Jesus; young women need to be close to their fathers to have a significant effect on their image of Mary and Jesus.

TABLE 4.6

God as Mother/Lover by Closeness to Parents by Sex
(Percent in top quartile)

	Men	Women
Very close to neither	29	39
Very close to mother	28	37
Very close to father	18	36
Very close to both	37	32

For young men closeness to both parents is needed in order to notably improve the strength of their image of God as a mother and a lover. For the young women, however, closeness to either parent bears little relationship to their image of God.

There are three different patterns of relationship in the family triad, one for Jesus, one for Mary, and one for God. In general it can be said that for young men what really is important in enhancing all three of their images is to be close to both parents; for young women, to enhance their stories of Jesus and Mary it is necessary for them to be close to their fathers. Closeness to both parents enhances somewhat young women's story of grace.

A joyous approach to religion, as one might imagine, in both parents also affects whether there is joy in the religious imagination of young people (Table 4.7). It seems to be important for young men that both parents be joyous; for young women closeness to one parent is sufficient (presumably the father, though our scale does not permit us to determine this). Stories of God, it would appear, are told in interpersonal relation to children by both parents, and especially by the father, if the child is a daughter.

TABLE 4.7

Grace Scale by Family Religious Joy
(Percent in top quartile)

Joy	Men	Women
Low	16	24
Medium	19	34
High	25	32

There is no negative impact on the grace story by the mother pursuing a career or holding a job. Indeed there is some reason to believe (Table 4.8) that a working mother actually enhances a young woman's story of grace. (In a subsequent chapter we will see that working mothers tend to have less close relationships with their daughters. However, the closeness of a woman's relationship with her daughter does not have much impact on her religious imagination, which is shaped more by the father.)

TABLE 4.8

Grace Scale by Whether Mother Worked During Infancy, Childhood, Teens
(Percent in top quartile)

	Men	Women
Did not work	17	27
One period	27	32
Two periods	18	39
All three periods	16	32

It is very important for the development of a young man's religious imagination that he perceives his parents as close to one another when he is growing up (Table 4.9). Twenty-four percent of those young men who said their parents are very close are in the top quartile of the grace scale as opposed to 10 percent of those who said their parents were not too close. It is also important for a young woman, although here the difference is between 34 percent and 24 percent. Closeness to both parents for a son, closeness to a father for a daughter, and a closeness of parents to one another for children of both sexes seem to be the ingredients in the family triad necessary for a young person to receive an image of loving goodness that will modify the religious imagination.

TABLE 4.9

Grace Scale by Relationship Between Parents by Sex
(Percent)

Parents were:	Men	Women
Very close	24	34
Pretty close	17	27
Not too close	10	24

The exercise of authority in the family, however, seems to make little difference in the religious imagination of either son or daughter (Table 4.10). It does not much matter whether the mother or the father makes decisions about the children and executes punishment, though there is some slight improvement if the parents act together.

TABLE 4.10

Grace Scale by Family Authority Structure
(Percent in top quartile)

	Who punished	Who made decisions
Father	23	22
Mother	23	24
Both	26	26

The religious devotion of parents has an effect on the religious imagination of their children. Men are almost completely unaffected by their father's communion reception and strongly affected by their mother's. Women seem to be affected by the communion reception of both parents—somewhat less by their mother's than by their father's. For men the impact comes from a weekly communicant mother and from a father who goes at least several times a month. For women the impact is also from a weekly communicant mother and especially from a more than weekly communicant father. All our respondents were more likely to have a "graceful" religious imagination if at least one parent was a weekly communicant regardless of the respondent's sex (Tables 4.11, 4.12, pages 56-57).

TABLE 4.11

Grace Scale by Father's Communion by Sex
(Percent in top quartile)

	Men	Women
More than weekly	20	38
Weekly	19	37
2–3 times a month	20	26
Less	14	23

Which way does the causal influence flow in the relationships we have discussed thus far? It is unlikely that a more graceful story of God will incline a young person to a more gracious memory of childhood relationships (though it is not impossible). It is also unlikely that a more graceful story of God will lead young adults to remember the devotion of their parents in a more favorable light. Hence it seems reasonable to say that devout parents who are joyous and close to one another and their children do indeed play the role of "sacrament," mediating between the loving goodness which is purported to exist beyond the human condition and the perception of that loving goodness by their children. In the case of young women, the father's impact is especially important.

TABLE 4.12

Grace Scale by Mother's Communion by Sex
(Percent in top quartile)

	Men	Women
More than weekly	31	39
Weekly	29	32
2–3 times a month	17	32
Less	17	28

TABLE 4.13

Perception of Parents' Religious Effect and Grace Scale by Sex
(Percent in top quartile)

	MEN		WOMEN	
	Father	Mother	Father	Mother
Very much	21	24	25	30
Some	16	16	28	26
Not too much	16	16	20	16
Not at all	10	14	25	25

Do our respondents perceive this parental influence we have described? In one of our questions we asked them how much their mother and their father influenced them religiously.

Survey Question

(Circle one number beside each category)

	Very much	Some	Not too much	Not at all	This category does not apply to me
A. Religion classes in Catholic school	1	2	3	4	5
B. Religion classes for public school children	1	2	3	4	5
C. My mother	1	2	3	4	5
D. My father	1	2	3	4	5
E. My spouse	1	2	3	4	5
F. My friends	1	2	3	4	5
G. My parish community	1	2	3	4	5
H. Retreats, encounter groups, discussion or prayer groups	1	2	3	4	5
I. Reading on my own	1	2	3	4	5
J. Sermons at Mass	1	2	3	4	5
K. Talking with a priest, brother, or nun	1	2	3	4	5

Men who remember both their mothers and their fathers having important religious influence on them have higher scores on the grace scale than men who do not have such recollection. Curiously enough, the highest score on the grace scale comes from women who remember their mothers having very much religious influence on them, and there is no pattern of relation between the religious imagination and recollection of father's influence. We have already noted, however, that fathers do affect the religious imagination of daughters quite substantially. We might conclude from Table 4.13 (page 57) that young women do not perceive this impact, perhaps because the dynamics by which it is achieved are so subtle.

All the variables we have considered correlate significantly (Table 4.14, page 59) with the religious imagination. A factor combining the seven variables has a .21 correlation with the grace condition of the religious imagination, exactly the same correlation that exists between the grace scale and religious experience. In other words, as important as our direct experiences of hope-renewing goodness are, they are no more important than the ordinary experiences of family life.

TABLE 4.14

Correlations Between Grace Scale and Family Background Variables
(Coefficient of Correlation = Pearson's r)

Close to parents	.09
Mother-father relationship	.10
Family joy	.13
Mother's communion	.08
Father's influence	.17
Mother's influence	.12
Combined family factor	.21

Furthermore, these two influences are relatively independent of one another. When family, nature, and experience are put into a multiple regression equation (Table 4.15), there is some diminution of strength of the correlation of each variable, but all remain significant and all have their own independent direct effect on the religious imagination, an effect which is illustrated in Figure 4.1 (page 58), in which we see that while sensitivity to nature and religious experience relate to each other, the quality of family life, in fact, relates neither to sensitivity to nature nor to a propensity to religious experience. (In other research, McCready and I have demonstrated that a "very joyous" religious style in the father does indeed correlate with certain kinds of religious experience. That relationship, however, is submerged in the combinations of variables into the scales used in Figure 4.1). This is a finding we will encounter repeatedly in the present book. The various "sacraments" which reveal loving goodness to a young person exercise mostly independent effects, cumulating in a heightened grace effect.

TABLE 4.15

Correlations With Grace Scale

	r	Beta
Family	.21	.17
Nature	.16	.12
Experience	.21	.17

FIGURE 4.1

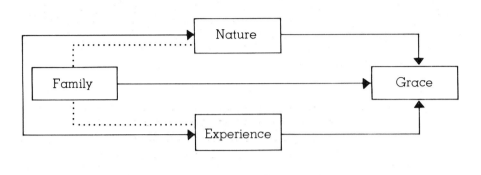

In conclusion, we can say there are four different ways the family or origin affects the religious imagination of one of its offspring: 1) the relationship between the parents of the child, both parents for the son, especially the father for the daughter; 2) the relationship of the parents to one another; 3) the religious devotion of both parents, especially if they are very devout; 4) the perception by the child of the parent as religious influential, which presumably indicates the parent's explicit attempt to teach religion. (The lack of daughters' perception of their father's influence on them religiously perhaps reflects the fact that fathers do not often teach religion explicitly; they do so more by their actions, perhaps, than by their words.)

McCready points out that early childhood studies have shown that very small children begin their observations with long periods of what is called "steady staring":

> At first the researchers thought these children were handicapped in some ways because they stared as though fixated at an object for long periods of time, maybe several minutes. However, gradually the research concludes that the children were simply absorbing reality in a very intense manner.

One might conclude from this that small children spend a great deal of time steadily staring at the adults around them as well. They want to see how the adults treat each other, and this information is used by the child to form an opinion as to whether the grown-up world is benign or not. It is a great mistake on the part of many parents to assume that their children don't know what's going on in the family or don't know what the parents are talking about, particularly if they are fighting. Children read body language and voice tones very, very well, and are not easily fooled by parents who think that "Children don't know what's going on." Children have very little to do all day except to observe the world around them, and therefore they pick up the ambiance of the family quite quickly, and sometimes, even though they can't verbalize it, they become the strongest critics of the family unit.

The religious issue at this stage of life is whether or not one can learn to trust in the graciousness of reality. Trust stems from what the children see in their parents' life and in the context within which they are raised. If they see violence or capriciousness or inconsistent treatment or discipline, they will have trouble developing a belief in the goodness of the world. They will not grow in trust.[1]

Parents are storytellers. They are telling the story of their own lives and of the romance, with its ups and downs, of their life together. We are incurable lovers of story ("Mommy, tell me a story!", according to Nathan Scott, is the primal cry of all humankind for meaning in life). Children watch in fascination the story their parents are telling. The underlying theme of hope or despair, of graciousness or absurdity which runs through the parental story is surely communicated with the main themes of the stories. Dumas Père and Fils are by no means the only parent-child relationship which produced storytelling. The religious imagination of young people is powerfully influenced by what goes on in the family of origin. Other factors, as we shall see, make their contribution too; but they are building on a foundation that the family has laid.

If parents ask when are they affecting the religious imagination of our children, the answer is: All the time.

NOTES

[1]William C. McCready, "The Synod and Family Dynamics: Issues in Religious Socialization," unpublished paper, NORC, pp. 5-6.

Highlights

1   There are virtually no correlations between the grace scale and formal education or years of Catholic schooling or years of CCD (Table 5.1).

2   It is clear that it is not the time spent in religious education that impacts on the religious imagination but rather the nature of the instructional relationship between teacher and student (Tables 5.3, 5.4).

3   The quality of instruction affects most measures of religious devotion at least as powerfully as the number of years of religious education (Table 5.5).

4   The content which seems to have the most influence on the religious imagination deals with love, Jesus, relationships, and other persons (Table 5.6).

5   There is a high correlation between love, Jesus, relationships, other persons, and the opinion of young people on the quality of their religious instruction (Tables 5.7, 5.8).

6   The relationship between the quality of instruction and a gracious religious story for CCD students is almost entirely a matter of educational techniques; for those who have gone to Catholic schools the techniques affect the religious imagination through their impact on the quality of the instruction (Table 5.9, Figure 5.1).

7   It is not the quantity of the education that matters but the quality; it is the relationship with an excellent teacher that affects the religious imagination.

Chapter 5

Religious Education

In this chapter we turn to the impact of formal religious instruction on the religious imagination. The correlations between the grace scale and formal education or years of Catholic schooling or years of CCD is virtually zero (Table 5.1). Nor is there any difference at all on the grace scale between those who have had some Catholic instruction and those who have had none. Neither of these findings is unexpected, for it was hypothesized at the beginning that religious stories are transmitted through relationships, and that experiences of grace are mediated through people and not through formal propositions. It may well be that a specific, especially gifted, devout, or attractive teacher as a person can be a "sacrament of grace," but classrooms as such, whatever their merit (and it is not my intention to deny those merits), are not likely to have much effect on the imagination.

TABLE 5.1

Correlation Between Grace Scale
and Formal Education
(Coefficient of Correlation = Pearson's r)

Educational attainment	.00
Years of Catholic school	.01
Years of CCD	.02

TABLE 5.2

Grace Scale by Whether Respondent Had
Any Religious Instruction At All
(Percent in top quartile)

None	22
Some	22

It is possible to measure the impact of an able teacher. Our respondents were asked first of all to rate the quality of the instruction in Catholic schools and in CCD both in grammar school and high school (Table 5.3). Of those who attended Catholic grammar school 12 percent said the instruction was excellent, and 40 percent said it was excellent or very good. The comparable numbers for grammar school CCD were 7 percent and 27 percent. At the high school level, the percentages are virtually the same, 17 percent and 45 percent for Catholic high schools, 8 percent and 27 percent for CCD. There are statistically significant correlations between the grace scale and the quality of instruction for both Catholic schools and CCD (Table 5.4). What matters in both educational contexts is not the number of years of participation but rather the quality of religious instruction which occurs during that time. It is not the number of hours or years spent in the classroom but the nature of the instructional relationship between teacher and student.

TABLE 5.3

Quality of Catholic Religious Instruction
(Percent)

	GRAMMAR SCHOOL		HIGH SCHOOL	
	Catholic School	CCD	Catholic School	CCD
Excellent	12	7	17	8
Very Good	40	27	45	27

TABLE 5.4

Correlations Between Grace Scale and Quality of Catholic Education
(Coefficient of Correlation = Pearson's r)

	GRAMMAR SCHOOL		HIGH SCHOOL	
	Catholic School	CCD	Catholic School	CCD
Grace	.11	.19	.13	.17

When the grammar school and high school scales are combined (Table 5.5, page 67), there is a .21 relationship between quality of instruction in Catholic schools and the religious imagination and a .08 relationship between CCD participation and a gracious religious imagination. (These correlations can only apply to those who attended both Catholic grammar school and high school or both grammar school and high school CCD. In both instances relatively small proportions of the population fit that description. For further discussion on why young people do not participate in religious instruction classes, particularly at the high school level, and also of the importance of the quality of instruction on religious devotion, see the pertinent chapter in *The Young Catholic Adult.*) The quality of instruction affects not only the religious imagination but also most measures of religious devotion at least as powerfully as does sheer number of years of educational participation.

TABLE 5.5

**Correlations Between Grace Scale and
Quality of Education Scale**
(Coefficient of Correlation = Pearson's r)

	Catholic Schools	CCD
Grace	.21	.08*

* Not statistically significant.

The question naturally arises as to what defines the quality of religious instruction. It does not seem to matter, according to my analysis, whether the teachers are lay or religious nor whether there are outside activities (Table 5.6, page 69). Four kinds of religious instruction do seem to correlate with young people's estimates that they have received excellent religious instruction. These deal with 1) how to live in today's world, 2) loving Christianity, 3) the life of Jesus, 4) the value of personhood.

Survey Questions

Religion classes vary in what they teach. Think about the classes you have attended in *high school.*

If you have ever attended a Catholic high school, answer "A."

If you have ever attended Religious Education classes for public high school students, answer "B."

If you have attended both Catholic high school and Religious Education classes for public high school students, answer "A" *and* "B."

A. Did your Catholic high school classes teach each of the following?

	Yes	No
(1) Scripture, the old and new testaments of the Bible	1	2
(2) How to live in today's world	1	2
(3) General ideas about love and Christianity	1	2
(4) The life of Jesus	1	2
(5) Catholic doctrine, the meaning of the sacraments, grace, etc.	1	2
(6) The writings of Catholic theologians like St. Augustine, St. Thomas Aquinas, etc.	1	2
(7) The value of personhood	1	2
(8) What it means to be a Catholic	1	2

Which one of these things did your Catholic high school classes spend the most time on?

B. Did your religious education classes teach each of the following?

	Yes	No
(1) Scripture, the old and new testaments of the Bible	1	2
(2) How to live in today's world	1	2
(3) General ideas about love and Christianity	1	2
(4) The life of Jesus	1	2
(5) Catholic doctrine, the meaning of the sacraments, grace, etc.	1	2
(6) The writings of Catholic theologians like St. Augustine, St. Thomas Aquinas, etc.	1	2
(7) The value of personhood	1	2
(8) What it means to be a Catholic	1	2

Which one of these things did your religious instruction classes spend the most time on?

Education on how to live in today's world and personhood seem to be the most powerful correlates for those who went to Catholic schools; the life of Jesus is the most important for those who went to CCD. Love and Christianity seems to correlate at an equal level with esteem for the quality of instruction in both educational contexts. Whatever is to be said about the personal attributes of the teachers, certain content material seems to have an impact on the religious imagination; the material, be it noted, all deals with love, with Jesus, with relationships, and with persons—subject matter with high imaginative resonance.

TABLE 5.6

Correlations With Quality Education
(Coefficient of Correlation = Pearson's r)

	Catholic Schools	CCD
Outside activities	.00	.09
How to live in today's world	.25	.08
Love and Christianity	.17	.19
Life of Jesus	.12	.31
Value of personhood	.25	.13

Both religious education contexts seem to be placing considerable emphasis on these four important subject matters (Table 5.7, page 70), though Catholic schools are somewhat more likely to stress the life of Jesus and the value of personhood. When these four measures are combined into a scale correlating "educational quality index" and "Instruction techniques" and this scale in turn is related to the estimation young people have of the quality of the religious education they have received, we find (Table 5.8, page 70) a very powerful relationship (.35 for Catholic schools and .29 for CCD). Emphasis on these four subject matters, in other words, plays a considerable part in determining whether young people think they have received high quality religious instruction.

Do the instructional techniques have an effect of their own independent of whether they have shaped the young person's evaluation of the quality of his religious education (an evaluation which in all likelihood describes the quality of the relationship with his teacher)? Here the answer is different for Catholic schools and CCD (Tables 5.9, Figure 5.1, pages 70-71). The subject matter of instruction influences the grace scale equally in both CCD and Catholic school contexts (.11). However, when the quality of instruction variable is entered, the instructional technique becomes unimportant for Catholic schools and remains statistically significant for CCD. The relationship, in other words, between the quality of instruction and a gracious religious story for CCD students is almost entirely a matter of educational techniques, whereas the educational techniques have their effect for those who have gone to Catholic schools through their impact on the evaluation of the quality of religious instruction. This leads one to conclude—very, very tentatively—that the technique of instruction for CCD (and "technique of instruction" here means the substantive matters discussed) is even more important for those Catholics (378 of our respondents) who have had at least some CCD instruction at the grammar and high school level than it is for 25 percent of our respondents who have had at least some Catholic schooling at the grammar and high school level.

TABLE 5.7

Teaching Activities Which Correlate With Educational Quality Index
(Percent "Yes")

	Catholic Schools	CCD
How to live in today's world	77	72
Love and Christianity	93	90
Life of Jesus	80	71
Value of personhood	71	63

TABLE 5.8

Correlation With Quality Measure and "Instructional Techniques"
(Coefficient of Correlation = Pearson's r)

	Catholic Schools	CCD
Net of quality of instruction	.35	.29

TABLE 5.9

Correlations Between "Grace" and Instructional Technique Scales
(Percent)

	Catholic Schools	CCD
r	.11	.11
Beta	.03*	.11

* Not statistically significant.

FIGURE 5.1

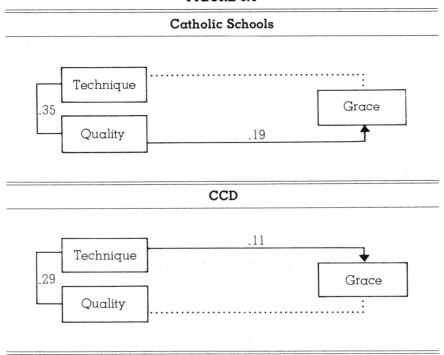

Catholic Schools

CCD

Given the climate of controversy which exists in the Catholic Church about the two forms of religious instruction, it is difficult to say anything on the subject which is not controversial and which will not offend either one side or the other. However, presumably one is on safe ground to say that the quality of religious instruction (which in part is a matter of subject matter, particularly subject matter that deals with relationships) is important in both contexts and can have an impact on the religious imagination in both contexts. One must add that the quality of instruction is rated higher in Catholic schools and that the correlation between the quality of instruction in grammar school and high school in the grace scale is higher for those who have had the Catholic school experience. Nonetheless, the quality of instruction does have an impact in both educational settings.

However, one can offend both groups by observing that only 12 percent of those who attended Catholic grammar school and 17 percent of those who attended Catholic high schools rate the quality of their instruction as excellent. The figures for CCD are 7 percent and 8 percent respectively. There is enormous room for improvement in Catholic instruction in both the school and CCD contexts.

The policy implications of these data are obvious for those involved in any kind of Catholic religious instruction. It must be clear that questions of finances, administration organization, theories of what ought to be taught, are of considerably less importance than the quality of the religious instruction and the quality of the relationship between teacher and student.

Finally, of those 300 respondents who have had some Catholic grammar and high school experience (Table 5.10), the quality of Catholic education is not a mask of the influence of family or of sensitivity to nature or of religious experience. Indeed the beta of .21 is exactly the same as the r of .21 in Table 5.5 (page 67). The quality of instruction in Catholic school, then, like the other factors which shape the religious imagination, seems to have an independent effect.

TABLE 5.10

**Standardized Correlations Between Grace
and Background Variables**

(Betas)

Catholic quality	.21
Nature	.15
Experience	.20
Family	.14

The thesis that the religious imagination is shaped by relationships receives considerable support in this chapter. It is a relationship with the teacher, as specified by the student's evaluation of the quality of the teaching, and subject matter that deals with the relational dimensions of human living that shape the religious imagination. It is these and not the repetition of propositional doctrine or the number of years of education which contribute to a gracious and graceful story of the meaning of life.

Does school matter in the shaping of the religious imagination? It matters more than one might have expected. For the one quarter of our young adults who had some Catholic grammar school and some Catholic high school, school matters as much as does family and religious experience. For the little more than one quarter who had both some grammar and some high school CCD, their religious instruction does matter somewhat in the shaping of their religious imagination. It is not quantity of the education that matters, but the quality. The religious imagination is shaped especially in those circumstances (quite infrequent by the judgment of our young adults) when the quality of religious instruction is excellent. It is the relationship with an excellent teacher rather than the fact of or the duration of attendance in religious instruction programs that affects the religious imagination.

The Friendship Variable

Highlights

1   *The impact of friends on the religious imagination is seen in the responses to two questions: How much can you learn about life from talking with friends, and how much have friends affected the way you think about the Catholic faith?*

2   *In both cases (Tables 6.3, 6.4) those who give strong credit to the influence of friends are more likely to be in the top quarter in the grace scale. This influence is positive rather than negative.*

3   *It is a more powerful factor for women than for men (Tables 6.5, 6.6), perhaps because in contemporary American culture men are somewhat less likely to discuss religion seriously with each other.*

4   *When correlations are standardized (Table 6.8), the friendship factor is somewhat less important than family or religious experience and about as important as sensitivity to nature in influencing the development of the person's religious story.*

5   *The combination of Catholic education—either of some duration or of high quality—and the influence of friends produces a notable impact on the development of the religious imagination (Table 6.9).*

Chapter 6

The Friendship Variable

While the family may be expected to have a powerful influence on the development of the religious imagination, particularly in early life, as time goes on the child becomes an adolescent and the pressures of the peer group can also be expected to have religious influence. Often, one supposes, the peer group pressures are negative, but it is not impossible that friends also have a positive religious impact. Two questions in our survey enabled us to examine the impact of friends on the religious imagination.

TABLE 6.1

Learning the Meaning of Life From Friends For Young Catholics
(Percent)

Great deal	40
Some	41
Little	17
None	2
Total	100

TABLE 6.2

Friends Affected Catholic Faith for Young Catholics
(Percent)

Very much	11
Some	40
Not too much	49

The first ["Here are some ways of learning about life and the forces governing it. . . . how much (can) you learn about life from talking with friends?"] deals with the meaning of life and the forces governing it. The second asks an explicit question about the Catholic faith ["How much has each of the following affected the way you think about the Catholic faith? (D) my friends (circle one) very much, some, not too much, not at all, this category does not apply to me]. About 40 percent say they learned a great deal about the meaning of life from their friends, and 11 percent say that friends have affected their Catholic faith "very much." In both cases (Tables 6.3 and 6.4, pages 76), those who give strong credit to friends for their influence are much more likely to be in the top quartile in the grace scale. Thirty-three percent of those who say friends had great influence in shaping their views of the meaning of life and 41 percent of those who say their friends have a great deal of influence on what they think about Catholicism are also in the top quartile of the grace scale. Indeed, those who say their friends have had "very much" influence on their Catholicism are twice as likely to be in the top quartile of the grace scale as those who say their friends had "not too much" or "none at all" influence. Friends, then, do have a considerable religious influence in shaping the religious imagination. It would appear that the influence is positive rather than negative (Tables 6.3, 6.4). It is also a more powerful factor for women than for men (Tables 6.5 and 6.6, page 77). Fully half the women who say their friends have very much influence on their Catholicism are on the top half of the grace scale. The impact may be less on men because in contemporary American culture men are somewhat less likely to discuss religion seriously with each other. Thirty-five percent of the men, as opposed to forty-five percent of the women, say that they learned a good deal about the meaning of life from their friends.

TABLE 6.3

Grace and Friends' Influence on the Meaning of Life
(Percent in top quartile)

Friends had great influence	33
Some influence	22
Little influence	18

TABLE 6.4

Grace and Friends' Religious Impact
(Percent in top quartile)

Very much	41
Some	29
Not too much	23
Not at all	21

TABLE 6.5

Grace and Friends' Influence on Meaning by Sex
(Percent in top quartile)

	Men	Women
Great	27	37
Some	16	27
Little	15	21

TABLE 6.6

Grace and Friends' Religious Impact by Sex
(Percent in top quartile)

	Men	Women
Very much	27	51
Some	24	33
Not much	18	25

When the two "friends" items are combined into a single "friendship" factor the correlation between this factor and the grace scale is .19, an influence of the same sort as family and religious experience in shaping the religious imagination (Table 6.7). When the correlations are standardized (Table 6.8), the friendship factor is somewhat less important than family or religious experience and about as important as sensitivity to nature in influencing the development of a gracious religious imagination.

TABLE 6.7

Correlation Between Grace and Friendship Factor
(Coefficient of Correlation = Pearson's r)

Correlation	.19

TABLE 6.8

Standardized Correlations For Influences on "Grace" Scale
(Betas)

Nature	.12
Family	.17
Religious experience	.16
Friends	.11

One can begin to imagine now the religious imagination growing in "layers," as the "stories" of God are told to a maturing individual by various sources—the powers of nature, religious experience, school, and friends. Each of these seems to make a relatively independent and relatively equal impact on the development of the person's religious story, at least insofar as the story can be measured by our scale.

Where are people likely to encounter friends who will have positive effects on their religious imagination? One of the places surely seems to be Catholic schools. Sixty-four percent of those respondents who have had more than 7 years of Catholic education and who have been highly influenced by their friends are at the top half of the grace scale (Table 6.9), and 71 percent of those who report "high quality" religious education and high influence by friends are at the top half of the grace measure.

TABLE 6.9

Influence of Friends on Grace by Years of Catholic Education

(Percent in top half of "Grace" scale)

Friends Influence (Factor)	Less than 7 yrs. of Catholic School	More than 7 yrs. of Catholic School
(high	51 N = (108)	64 N = (42)
to	43 N = (289)	36 N = (78)
low)	36 N = (67)	28 N = (7)

Thus the combination of Catholic education, either of some duration or of high quality, and influence of friends produces a notable impact on the development of the religious imagination (although there is no certainty from our data that the friends are in fact people our respondents attended school with).

The focus of our research in the young adult study was not on the development of the religious imagination but on other and different matters. Our religious education interest was, in a certain sense, "piggybacked" on the primary concern of the clients and the research staff. It now seems evident, however, that if further study is done directly on the religious imagination, many more explicit questions need to be asked about the kinds and qualities of the relationships we have seen thus far affecting the religious imagination. We would want to know more about the teachers who gave high quality instruction and more about the friends who seem to have had such a benign influence. At what age was this influence, how was it exercised—through friends of the same sex or the opposite sex? What were the circumstances and the conditions under which the influence was felt? This book will not address those questions; its purpose is to report the preliminary reconnaissance which indicates that one can say with confidence that friends as well as family are "sacraments of grace," beings whose loving goodness reveal the possibility of even greater loving goodness at work underpinning the cosmos. Any human institution concerned about propagating stories of grace must realize that it is dealing not with isolated individuals, but rather with persons caught in dense relational networks, and then that one is most likely to have influence on the individual person when one is also influencing the whole network. To use the storytelling metaphor, one tells the story to a whole audience, and to some extent the success of the story is mediated through the reaction of the audience. If your friends happen to enjoy the story, then you are more likely to enjoy it, too.

TABLE 6.10

Influence of Friends on "Grace" by Quality of Catholic Education
(Percent in top half of "Grace" Scale)

Friends Influence Factor	No Catholic School	Quality Low	Quality High
(high	53	58	71
	N = (158)	N = (36)	N = (31)
to	45	35	53
	N = (405)	N = (92)	N = (30)
low)	34	13	50
	N = (164)	N = (15)	N = (6)

The Effect of the Parish

Highlights

1 *A very substantial number of Catholics say that their attitude towards their religion has been shaped by their parish or parish-related organizations and activities.*

2 *Ironically, while only a small percent rate the sermons as excellent, the sermon is the simple most important parish activity in affecting the attitudes towards Catholicism. If sermons have any influence at all, it is a positive one (Table 7.1).*

3 *An active parish, the pastor's performance, and lay influence also correlate positively and have influence on the religious imagination of the young adult (Tables 7.5–7.7).*

4 *Ascetical practices (retreats, days of recollection, spiritual reading, etc.) correlate highly on the "grace" scale. It does not seem possible to argue that asceticism influences the development of the religious imagination since it is, at least in part, a result of the religious imagination (Table 7.8).*

5 *The sermon factor sums up everything else the parish does; nothing else matters if the sermon is not good. Sermons have an independent influence of their own (Table 7.9) as strong as family and nature and Catholic schooling. It appears that the quality of sermons increases the impact of the quality of Catholic education.*

6 *The varied influences on the religious imagination have an "overlapping" function—which means that the person is more likely to have a benign story of God and of life if experience and nature cooperate, if experience and the quality of sermons cooperate, etc. (Tables 7.10–7.17).*

Chapter 7

The Effect of the Parish

The friendship network which may have shaped the religious imagination could exist either in the past or the present, but the parish community is a present reality, one which is "layered on" to the previous determinants of the religious imagination—experience, nature, family, friends, and school (and, if a person is married, spouse). The typical modern American parish is large, busy, allegedly impersonal, and frequently less than satisfying to younger and better educated Catholics. Can it make any contribution to the further shaping of the religious imagination?

First of all, how do our young Catholics rate their parish? Only 14 percent think sermons are excellent, though a little better than 50 percent think they are excellent or good (Table 7.1, page 84). A little more than a third think that priests are very understanding, and a little less than a third say that laity have a great deal of influence in the parish. Forty percent describe their parish as active, but 80 percent are willing to approve their pastor's performance. Surprisingly enough, given the criticisms describing the sermon, the influence of the laity, and the sympathy of priests as imperfect, a very substantial number of Catholics say that their attitude towards their religion has been shaped by their parish or parish-related organizations and activities. Thirty-six percent say that they have been affected either very much or some by their parish as such, 36 percent by discussion group and similar parish activities, 44 percent a conversation with a priest or a nun, and 52 percent say that their Catholicism has been affected either very much or some by sermons. There is considerable irony in the findings that only 14 percent of the young adults rate the sermons as excellent, but even under those circumstances the sermon is the single most important activity in affecting the attitudes towards Catholicism of the young adult—a point which parish priests would be very well advised to take seriously.

The importance of the sermon is conveyed by the relationship between the rating of the sermons and the young person's score on the "grace" scale. Forty percent of those who say the sermons are excellent are in the top quartile of the scale, as are 25 percent of those who say they are good, and only 15 percent of those who say the sermons are fair or poor (Table 7.2). All the other parish activities correlate with the "grace" scale—of those who say the priests are very sympathetic, 32 percent are in the top quartile, as are approximately 30 percent of those who say the parish community discussion groups, sermons, and conversations with priests have had a great deal of religious influence on them. Like friends, the parish has a positive influence when it has religious influence at all. Thus, while young people do not rate sermons very high, it is nonetheless true that the influence of the sermon is towards a higher score on the grace scale rather than a lower score. Sermons may turn people off, but if they have any influence at all, it is an influence in the positive direction, and as we learned in Table 7.2, excellent sermons seemed to have a very strong influence.

TABLE 7.1

The State of the Catholic Parish
(Percent)

Sermons excellent (or good)	58
Priest very understanding	36
Laity have a great deal of influence	30
Many parish activities	41
Approve of pastor's performance	81
Catholicism affected by:	
Parish [a]	36
Discussion groups, etc.	30
Sermons	52
Conversation with priest or nun	44
Three or more "ascetical" activities	20

[a] "very much or some"

TABLE 7.2

Sermons and "Grace"
(Percent in top quartile)

Sermons excellent	39
Good	25
Fair or poor	15

Furthermore, an active parish, approval of the pastor's performance, and lay influence in the parish also correlate positively with "gracious stories of God" (Tables 7.5—7.7, page 85).

Virtually each thing, then, that a parish does well seems to have its own influence on the religious imagination of the young adult.

TABLE 7.3

Sympathy of Parish Priest and "Grace"
(Percent in top quartile)

Very sympathetic	32
Fairly sympathetic	22
Not too sympathetic	21

TABLE 7.4

Influence on Catholic Faith of Community Activities and "Grace"
(Percent in top quartile on "Grace" Scale)

	Parish Community	Discussion Groups, etc.	Sermons	Conversation With Priest
Very much influence	30	33	28	29
Some influence	24	25	26	23
Not too much	21	26	18	20
None at all	17	17	12	17

TABLE 7.5

"Grace" and an "Active Parish"
(Percent in top quartile)

Very active	33
Pretty active	22
Not too active	15

TABLE 7.6

Grace and Satisfaction With Pastor's Performance
(Percent in top quartile)

Approve	26
Disapprove	17

TABLE 7.7

Grace and Amount of Lay Influence in Parish
(Percent in top quartile)

A lot	29
Some	22
Not much	12

Once again, however, we must face the question of the flow of causality. May it not be that those with a benign view of the meaning of life are more charitable in their evaluation of their priests and parishes, or are more likely to seek out competent priests and satisfying parishes, or might they not, finally, even be able to profit more from objectively mediocre performance than those who have a less positive and benign story of human life and of humankind's relationship with God?

All these possibilities are real and none of them can be readily excluded from our discussion. However, by the time the young adults come to their present parish community their religious imaginations have already been shaped by many other factors: religious experience, family, schools, friends. If those who are already disposed to be "gracious" in their evaluations of parish performance are doing so because of past effects of other agencies on their religious imagination, then the quality of parish performance might not be expected to add much of an influence of its own. If, on the other hand, the parish does make a contribution of its own to the development of their religious imagination above and beyond that made by agencies which have had prior influence, a persuasive case can be made that there is some causal flow from the parish to the religious imagination, and not vice versa. We will investigate this possibility in subsequent paragraphs.

First of all, however, it is worth noting that ascetical practices (Table 7.8, page 87) also have a considerable influence on the religious imagination. Retreats, days of recollection, spiritual readings, and other such matters correlate highly with the score on the "grace" scale: 56 percent of those who engage in five such practices being in the top quartile on the scale, as opposed to 17 percent of those who report no ascetical practices. In the case of ascetical practices, however, it does not seem possible to argue that the asceticism influences the development of the religious imagination since it is almost certainly, at least in part, a result of the religious imagination.

We constructed "factors" to measure the impact of the parish, one of them called "parish" loaded heavily on such matters as an active parish, lay influence in the parish, and the influence of parish community on one's Catholicism. The other factor, called "priests," loaded heavily on sermons, clerical sympathy and understanding, and influence of the priest on the person's religious life. As we note in Table 7.8A (page 87) both these factors have roughly the same predictive power as the simple question about the quality of the sermon. The quality of the sermon question is used in this analysis because it is as good an indicator as we have available for the influence of the parish community. The sermons sum up everything else the parish does; nothing else matters if the sermon is not very good.

TABLE 7.8

"Grace" and Asceticism [a]
(Percent)

No. of Ascetical Practices	Percent
0	17
1	24
2	26
3	33
4	36
5	56

[a] Retreats, days of recollection, spiritual reading, conversation with priest, etc.

TABLE 7.8A

Correlations Between Parish Scales and "Grace" Scale
(Coefficient of Correlation = Pearson's r)

	Sermons	Parish	Priest	Asceticism
Grace	.16	.20	.15	.14

Nor is the favorable reaction to Sunday sermons merely the result of religious imagination already shaped by family, friends, nature influence, and for those who have spent some time in Catholic elementary or high schools, by the influence of the quality of Catholic education. Sermons have an independent influence of their own (Table 7.9, page 89) of about the same order of magnitude as family and nature (and indeed, among those who have had some Catholic elementary and high school the quality of sermons *increases* the impact of the quality of Catholic education). It would appear, at least to some extent, that sermons do shape the religious imaginations after the shaping that has already been accomplished by prior institutions. When stories of God and the faith are constantly in process, each new positive influence that is brought to bear seems to be able to make a contribution of its own.

Tables 7.10—7.17 (pages 89-91) demonstrate this "overlapping" function of the varied influences on the religious imagination. The tables are so arranged that the percent in the upper left-hand corner always represents the proportion in the top quartile on the "grace" scale where both the two factors in the three-way table are positively correlated with the gracious response to otherness. In each instance whether it be nature and experience, experience and family, family and friends, friends and experience, sermons and friends, or sermons and religious experience, the quality of Catholic teaching and the importance of friends, and, finally, the quality of Catholic teaching and the quality of sermons, the score in the upper left-hand corner is always the highest, is always over 30 percent, and in all but two cases more than one-third of the respondents who fall in the area of where the two influences come together are in the upper quartile of the "grace" scale. It is also usually the case that only about 10 percent of those who are in the lower right-hand cell—that is to say, affected by neither of the two shaping variables—are in the top quartile on the "grace" scale. You are more likely, in other words, to have a benign story of God and of life if experience and nature cooperate, if experience and family cooperate, if family and friends cooperate, if friends and experience cooperate, if the quality of sermons and the quality of Catholic education cooperate, and if the influence of friends and quality of Catholic teaching cooperate. The highest proportion in the upper left-hand sector—37 percent in the top quartile—is to be found in Table 7.14, which measures the joint impact of sermons and friends. If one attempts a four-way table in which the influence on one's religious imagination of friends, religious experiences, and sermons are all taken into account, the upper left-hand cell which represents good sermons, religious experience, and friends with religious impact, fully two-fifths of the respondents in that sub-population are in the upper quartile—four times as many as those who are in the bottom right-hand cell of the table (where none of the three benign influences are at work). Table 7.15 shows neatly that each of the dynamics which tend to shape the religious imagination has an independent effect, so that as one moves from bottom to top and from right to left in the table, the proportion in the top quartile increases (save for the second cell on the left-hand side of the table, representing those respondents who have had religious experiences and who have been influenced by their friends; bad sermons undo to some extent the effect of the other two dynamics). Good sermons add fully fifteen percentage points to the proportion in the top quartile, even with the impact of friends and the prevalence of religious experiences held constant.

Another way of showing the accumulation of influence is to create a scale composed of the grace background variable—nature, religious experience, family, friends, sermons. Only about a tenth of those who have none or just one of those background variables are in the upper quartile on the religious imagination scale, whereas of those who have been affected by nature, have had religious experiences, have had a positive family background, have been influenced religiously by their friends, and have heard good sermons, more than half are in the top quartile of the grace scale. The religious imagination of the young adult has been shaped by a number of different influences, each one of which seems to make its own contribution to developing a benign view of Jesus, of Mary, of God, and of the hereafter.

TABLE 7.9

Standardized Correlations With Sources of "Grace" Scale
(Betas)

Nature	.09
Experience	.17
Family	.14
Friends	.16
Sermons	.11
Asceticism	.06
Quality of Catholic education	.23

TABLE 7.10

Grace by Experience by Nature
(Percent in top quartile)

	High	Low
Nature important	33	19
Not important	27	16

TABLE 7.11

Grace by Experience by Family
(Percent in top quartile)

	High	Low
Family warm	33	18
Not warm	25	12

TABLE 7.12

Grace by Family by Friends
(Percent in top quartile)

	Family Warm	Family Not Warm
Friends religiously important	30	21
Not important	19	11

TABLE 7.13

Grace by Friends by Experience
(Percent in top quartile)

	Friends Important	Friends Not Important
Experience high	34	21
Experience low	22	13

TABLE 7.14

Grace, Friends, Sermons
(Percent in top quartile)

	Friends Important	Friends Not Important
Sermons good	37	18
Sermons bad	23	13

TABLE 7.15

Grace, Friends, Religious Experience and Sermons
(Percent in top quartile)

	Friends Important	Friends Not Important
Experiences High		
Sermons good	42	27
Sermons bad	27	17
Experiences Low		
Sermons good	34	14
Sermons bad	14	10

TABLE 7.16

Grace by Quality of Catholic Teaching by Importance of Friends
(Percent in top quartile)

	Friends Important Religiously	Friends Not Important Religiously
Catholic school quality high	31	4
Catholic school quality low	14	3

Yet another way of expressing the same phenomenon is to use a multiple regression equation in which each of the variables is added successively to see how much each contributes to explaining variance (Table 7.19, page 92). The multiple R for the equation is .34 (thus succeeding Professor Sidney Verba's standard "reality"). Each of the variables makes its own additional or layered contribution to the variants explained of either two or three percentage points; that is to say, each new variable adds either two or three points to the R^2. An important contribution is made by each one of the dynamisms that influence the religious imagination of about the same size as it is added to the story of a person's life.

TABLE 7.17

Grace by Quality of Catholic School by Quality of Sermon
(Percent in top quartile)

Catholic School Quality	Sermons Good	Sermons Poor
High	34	17
Low	26	7

TABLE 7.18

Grace Scale by Number of Grace Background Variables [a]
(Percent in top quartile)

No. of Variables	
0	13
1	10
2	19
3	37
4	39
5	53

[a] The five grace background variables were nature, religious experience, family, friends, and sermons.

One might say that the religious imagination not only provides a story of God but is itself the subject of a story as it develops in the course of a young adult's life, and then one can trace the story of the development of the religious imagination.

The model for those attending Catholic grammar school and high school at least some of the time is even more interesting. The mutiple R goes up to .55 and almost a third of the variance is explained. Once high-quality Catholic education is introduced into shaping the religious imagination, then high-quality sermons make a substantial additional contribution to influence the imagination. Sermons add only two percent to the explained variance for the general population, but for those who have attended Catholic schools they add, in addition to the eleven point variance accounted for by high quality Catholic education, another ten points of explanatory power themselves. Quality Catholic schools and quality sermons triple the explanatory power of our model for those who have had at least some Catholic grammar school and high school education. Attendance at Catholic schools seems to dispose young people to be very considerably affected in their religious imagination by high quality teaching and high quality sermons.

TABLE 7.19

Variance Explained by Grace Experience Model

	All		Attended Catholic Schools	
	R	R^2	R	R^2
Nature	.18	.03	.18	.03
Experience	.24	.05	.24	.05
Family	.29	.08	.29	.08
Catholic School Quality	—	—	.43	.19
Sermons	.31	.10	.54	.29
Friends	.34	.12	.55	.30

These relationships may be expressed graphically in Figure 7.1 (page 93), which is the same as Figure 1.1. There are few indirect paths, only for statistically significant relationships inside the model: between experience and nature, between family background and sermons (so people from warmer and more religious backgrounds hear more in the sermons, are they more gracious in judging the sermons, or do they seek out better sermons?), between the impact of family and the impact of friends, and between the impact of nature and the impact of friends. The other five statistically significant paths in the model all go directly from a shaping dynamism to the grace scale, indicating that all five of the influences have a relatively dependent effect. The family exercises some of its influence through sermons and through friends, nature, and religious experiences; these affect one another, but most of the impact on the grace scale is direct and independent of other variables.

FIGURE 7.1

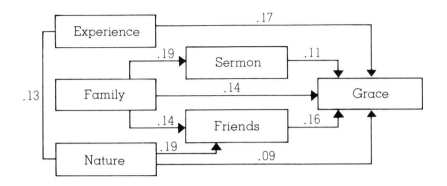

When one adds to the equation the quality of instruction in the Catholic schools (Figure 7.2, page 94), three additional dynamisms are added on to the model:

1. Catholic school quality has a direct influence of its own.

2. The impact of both sermons and friends is increased.

3. Religious experience now exercises its impact on religious imagination through its relationship with other variables.

If the quality of teaching is excellent, then the impact of other dynamisms on the development of the religious imagination is increased. However—and this should be kept clearly in mind since correlations predict low scores as well as high scores—if the quality of instruction in the school is poor, there will be lower scores on the grace scale. For the one quarter of the population which attends at least some Catholic grammar school and some Catholic high school, there is a gamble as far as the religious imagination goes. If the quality of instruction is excellent, or good, there is a much bigger payoff. If the quality of instruction is poor, then at least as far as the religious imagination goes, there can be a considerable negative influence.

There ought not to be much wonder about that. Five hours a day, five days a week, perhaps for sixteen years, of poor religious instruction can do enormous damage to the religious imagination—a point on which Catholic educators could do well to meditate before they congratulate themselves about the relationships demonstrated in Table 7.2. A high correlation means that the better the instruction the more influence will be exerted on the development of the young person's gracious story of God. But the poorer the instruction the more likely that the development of such a story will be impeded. Religious instruction in CCD may not have the possibility of such a strong pay-off on religious imagination, but neither does it have the possibility of such a negative effect if the quality of instruction is poor.

The hypotheses about the religious imagination, then, laid out in the first chapter have been sustained. It is influenced in a layered fashion by successive dynamics that work on the life of the young person, dynamics which are mostly relational. It is now essential to turn to the final relational dynamic, that of the spouse, for the one-third of our sample which is married.

FIGURE 7.2

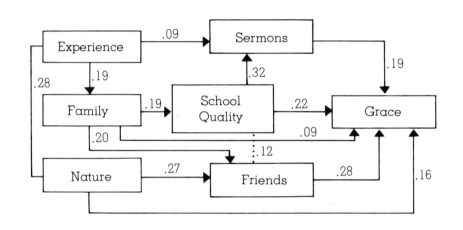

The Marriage Relationship

Highlights

1   Among married couples there is a strong correlation between a spouse's grace story and a respondent's grace story. If a spouse is high in his/her story of grace, the respondent is likely to be high (Table 8.1).

2   During the second five years of marriage the full impact of the stories which husbands and wives tell each other is seen—the gracious story of one spouse making likely the gracious story in the other.

3   The greatest agreement between husbands and wives at the top end of the grace scale is in the first two years of marriage and then in the final two years of the first decade of marriage (Table 8.2).

4   The strongest impact of religious storytelling seems to be the influence of husbands on wives, especially in the first decade of marriage.

5   The influence of spouses on each other's religious imagination is especially powerful when both are satisfied with their sexual relationship (Table 8.5).

6   A young adult's religious imagination is most likely to be gracious when he or she is married to a gracious and sexually fulfilling spouse. The combination of sexual fulfillment and a gracious story told by a spouse is especially powerful for women.

7   Religiously mixed marriages as such do not seem to affect the impact of spouses on each other's religious imagination (Table 8.6).

8   There is no more powerful dynamic affecting the religious imagination of an adult Catholic than the religious imagination of a spouse in a sexually fulfilling marriage.

9   The family of procreation is important in shaping religious imagination, especially after the first five years of marriage. This family is even more important if the sexual relationship of husband and wife is excellent.

Chapter 8

The Marriage Relationship

In both *The Young Catholic Family and Young Catholics* Survey, the NORC research team demonstrated the convergence of the religious imagination of husbands and wives and the influence of this convergence on their sexual fulfillment in marriage. The grace scale is strongly correlated (.8) with the warm religious imagination scale used in those previous works. The data to be reported in this chapter support these previous findings.

Some 400 respondents in the young adult study were married. Questionnaires were sent to the spouses of these people. It is possible therefore to analyze not only individuals but families. Presumably the husbands and wives filled out their questionnaires separately. There is no reason to expect they would conspire to give the same answers about their images of God, Jesus, Mary, and heaven. Nevertheless, there is a strong correlation between a spouse's grace story and a respondent's grace story. If such a spouse is high in his/her story of grace, then the respondent (Table 8.1, page 98) is 20 percentage points more likely to be in the top third of the grace scale. Moreover, as their relationship develops during the second five years of marriage (Table 8.2, page 98), if the spouse is low on the grace scale, then so is the respondent quite low on it; if the spouse is high, the respondent is twice as likely to be high on the scale as someone whose spouse is low. It takes time for the stories which husbands and wives tell each other to have their full impact.

Furthermore, the greatest agreement between husbands and wives at the top end of the scale is in the first two years of marriage and then in the final two years of the first decade of marriage. It is as though husbands and wives are confused about the religious stories they are telling one another in the intervening years of the decade, but by the final two years the stories clarify themselves. If your story is gracious, my story is twice as likely to be gracious. If your story is ungracious, my story is twice as likely to be ungracious.

TABLE 8.1

"Grace" Scale and Spouse's "Grace" Scale
(Percent in top third)

Spouse:	
Low	23
to	30
High	43

TABLE 8.2

Relationship Between Spouse's "Grace" and Own "Grace" by Duration of Marriage
(Percent in top third)

Spouse:	Less than 5 years	More than 5 years
Low	27	19
to	36	19
High	44	40

The strongest impact of the religious storytelling seems to be the influence of husbands on wives (Table 8.3). There is only eight percentage points difference between the men whose wives are high on the grace scale and those whose wives are low, while there is a twenty-five percentage point difference between the women whose husbands are high on the grace scale and those whose husbands are low on the grace scale. In other words, husbands seem to tell the story of grace more powerfully to their wives in the first decade of marriage than vice versa.

TABLE 8.3

Relationship Between "Grace" Scales by Duration of Marriage
(Percent in top third)

	0–2 yrs.	3–8 yrs.	9–10 yrs.
Low	44	17	22
to	50	25	24
High	56	36	50

The influence of spouses on each other's religious imagination is an especially powerful influence when both spouses are satisfied with their sexual relationship (Table 8.4, page 99). Indeed, if the sexual relationship is excellent and the spouse is high on the religious imagination scale, then 56 percent of the respondents also have a gracious religious imagination, as opposed to 39 percent in circumstances where one or both spouses does not consider the relationship excellent. A young adult's religious imagination is most likely to be gracious when he or she is in a situation where he or she is married to a gracious and sexually fulfilling spouse.

TABLE 8.4

Relationship Between Grace Scales by Sex of Respondent
(Percent in top third)

Spouse:	Men	Women
Low on "grace" scale	28	27
High on "grace" scale	36	52

The combination of sexual fulfillment and a gracious story told by a spouse is especially powerful for women (Table 8.5, page 100) which means they are almost twice as likely to be high on the grace scale (66 percent in the top third) if the sexual fulfillment in a marriage is excellent and if their spouse is telling a "gracious" story than is the case for men in the same circumstances. Sexual fulfillment and a gracious spouse influence both men and women's religious story, but women much more sharply and powerfully than men. The reasons for these apparent causals are quite beyond the analytic capability available to us by the present set of data. However, it may be that men take it for granted that their wives are pious and discount their piety to a considerable extent, even when they are sexually fulfilling partners. However, a woman not expecting piety in particular from a husband may well be greatly influenced by the combination of grace and passion suggested in Table 8.5.

The relationship between husbands and wives' stories of grace is .25 stronger for women than for men (almost twice as strong, .31 as opposed to .17, (Table 8.6, page 100) suggesting tht men influenced women more than the reverse. This influence is stronger in the second half of the first decade of marriage than in the first half (.31 versus .20), suggesting that the stories of grace converge as the years of marriage go by. It is much more powerful if the sexual fulfillment is excellent (.48) than when it is not excellent (.17). Religiously mixed marriages as such do not seem to affect the impact of spouses on each other's religious imagination. If one's spouse has a gracious story, in other words, it does not make much difference which denomination he or she may belong to.

TABLE 8.5

Relationship Between "Grace" Scales and Sexual Fulfillment in Marriage
(Percent in top third)

	Both Spouses Say Sex Is Excellent	One or Both Does Not Say Sex Is Excellent
Spouse:		
Low	12	17
to	36	29
High	56	39

TABLE 8.6

Relationship Between Grace Scales and Sexual Fulfillment by Sex of Respondent
(Percent in top third)

	Both "Excellent"		One or Both Not "Excellent"	
Spouse:	Men	Women	Men	Women
Low	16	14	33	23
High	37	66	29	40

One cannot emphasize enough the policy implication of the impact of sexual fulfillment on the relationship between husbands' and wives' religious stories. There is no more powerful dynamism affecting the religious imagination of an adult Catholic than the religious imagination of a spouse in a sexually fulfilling marriage. If the Church is interested in improving the quality of the religious imagination of its adults, the best way it could proceed would be to take steps to improve the quality of their sexual fulfillment. (When it is forced into it in passing, the Church does not seem to be very much involved in pursuing such a strategy!)

What happens if we add the spouse's influence to the explanatory models described in the previous chapter? The spouse, like the other five "layered" dynamisms, adds for all married respondents about 2 percent more to the R^2—that is to say, to the variance explained. There are, then, for Catholic adults six forces which shape their religious imagination, each one of which accounts for either two or three percent additional explanatory power when that layer of experience or relationship is added to the person's life.

TABLE 8.7

Correlations Between Own "Grace" and Spouse's "Grace"
(Coefficient of Correlation = Pearson's r)

Item	Correlation
Sex	
Men	.17
Women	.31
Duration of marriage	
0–5 years	.20
6–10 years	.31
Sexual fulfillment	
Both "excellent"	.48
One or both not excellent	.17
Mixed marriage	
Yes	.25
No	.24

However, if we look at those who have been married for more than five years (the second column of Table 8.8 (page 102), the explanatory power of the spouse is more than doubled. The R^2 goes from .14 to .17. The spouse now accounts for 5 percent additional explanatory power which means that after the first five years of marriage, the spouse becomes the most powerful influence on the religious imagination of an adult Catholic, and, indeed, is almost half as powerful in his/her impact on the religious imagination as all the prior variables put together. (The prior variables explain together 12 percent of the variance; the spouse adds 5 percent more.) Finally, when one looks at marriages in which both partners say that the sexual fulfillment is excellent, the explanatory power of the model is double, the R^2 increasing from .14 for all married respondents to .30 for those with sexually fulfilling relationships. The spouse in a sexually fulfilling relationship is more than twice as influential in shaping the religious imagination as all the prior influences put together. Each of the previous layers has accounted for 2 or 3 percent more explanatory power. But when one adds the spouse in a sexually fulfilling marriage, he or she contributes 18 percent more explanatory power—more than six times the explanatory power of any individual previous variable, and raises the variance explained from .12 for unmarried respondents and .14 for all married respondents to .30. Compared to the influence of a sexually fulfilling spouse who is telling a gracious story, all the other dynamisms that influence the religious imagination become unimportant. (The reverse is also true: that a sexually unfulfilling spouse, telling ungracious stories, has an enormous negative impact on the religious imagination).

TABLE 8.8

Variance Explained by Adding Spouse's "Grace" to Explanatory Model

	All Married Respondents	Married More Than 5 Yrs.	Both say Sex Excellent
R	.37	.41	.54
R^2	.14	.17	.30
R^2 Change	.02	.05	.18

Tables 8.9 and 8.10 (page 103) show the influence of the spouse (any spouse, not just the sexually fulfilling one) combined with sermons in 8.9 and friends in 8.10. Religiously influential friends and good sermons both make important contributions, as we know from previous chapters, to the development of the religious imagination. But, even if the sermons are excellent or good, a gracious spouse still accounts for sixteen percentage points of the proportion who are in the upper third on the religious imagination measure, and a gracious spouse compensates to some extent for poor or fair sermons. Similarly, a gracious spouse almost doubles the influence of religious friends if that influence was high, and more than doubles the influence if the friends have little influence. In short, sermons and friends are both important in shaping the religious imagination, but the graceful story told by the spouse makes a large addition to the impact both of the friendship group one knew presumably in one's younger years and to the religious community of the parish. The effectiveness is encapsulated in a respondent's reaction to the quality of the sermons. Combine a graceful story-telling spouse with good sermons and you have a very gracious religious imagination.

The family of procreation is the final imagination-shaping dynamism hypothesized at the beginning of this book. It makes an important additional contribution of its own over and above that made by the previous five layers. No matter what the circumstances of the marriage are, its contribution becomes notably more important after the first five years of the marriage and fantastically more important if the quality of the sexual relationship between husband and wife is excellent. There are not enough cases in our sample to look at situations in which we can combine influences of compelling sermons and the sexual fulfillment of the relationship. But we hardly need to push that one further analytic step—we have already proven beyond any doubt that the quality of marital intimacy converging and developing through the years of the marriage creates the religious story-telling milieu par excellence. It seems to be especially a story-telling milieu in which husbands influence wives, though the direction of the relationship flows both ways. If the story of grace is being told (presumably more in deed than in words) by a sexually fulfilling mate, the religious imagination will have a very gracious view of God, of heaven, of Jesus, and of Mary. To repeat policy advice given earlier: there seems to be no more effective way for a Church to facilitate the development of gracious religious imagination in its adult members than by striving to improve the quality of marital intimacy.

TABLE 8.9

"Grace" by Spouse's "Grace" by Sermon Quality
(Percent in upper third on grace scale)

Spouse Grace	Sermons Excellent or Good	Sermons Poor or Fair
Low	37	29
to	35	28
High	53	34

TABLE 8.10

"Grace" by Spouse's "Grace" by Influence of Friends
(Percent in upper third)

Spouse's Grace	Friend's Influence High	Friend's Influence Low
Low	27	12
to	40	24
High	53	32

Religion and the Life Cycle

Highlights

1   *The first life cycle phenomenon is the decline of religious devotion in the middle twenties followed by a rebirth particularly at the time of marriage in the late twenties.*

2   *The second life cycle phenomenon involves a slump in marital happiness between the second and eighth years, followed by a sharp rebound in the ninth or tenth year of marriage. This is called the "Kramer vs. Kramer" phenomenon.*

3   *This marital slump between the second and eighth years is paralleled by a slump in the "warmth" of the religious imagination; the rebound in sexual fulfillment in the ninth and tenth years is paralleled by a rebound in religious imagery.*

4   *While religious devotion fluctuates during the twenties, the religious imagination does not seem to do so (Tables 9.1, 9.2).*

5   *One's stories of God are unaffected by the alienation of the middle twenties or the reintegration at the end of the twenties, regardless of devotional practices or sexual attitudes (Tables 9.3, 9.4).*

6   *Religious devotion increases substantially as Catholics approach forty; 44 percent in their early thirties go to church weekly, 60 percent do so in their middle thirties, and 70 percent of those in their late thirties (Table 9.5).*

7   *The religious imagination of those alienated from the Church in the 1960s—at least those under thirty and very likely for those over thirty—has been unaffected by life cycle phenomena or by crises in the institutional Church (Table 9.7). The reason for the return of those alienated from the Church during the early 60s and early 70s, because of its sexual teaching, seems to be their ability to compartmentalize devotional Catholicism from sexual ethics.*

Chapter 9

Religion and Life Cycle

In two previous books, *The Young Catholic Family* and *Young Catholics*, my colleagues and I traced major life cycle phenomena that influence the religious lives of young Catholic adults. The first phenomenon is the decline of the religious devotion in the middle twenties, followed by a rebirth which occurs particularly at the time of marriage in the later twenties. We explained this decline as part of an alienation phenomenon which affected young adults' relationships with all social institutions followed by a reintegration which occurs with age and marriage towards the end of the twenties.

The second life cycle phenomenon, which we came to call the "Kramer vs. Kramer" phenomenon, involved a slump in marital happiness between the second and eighth years, followed by a very sharp rebound in the ninth and tenth years of the marriage. Furthermore, the marital slump was paralleled by a slump in the "warmth" in the religious imagination (as measured by a scale which is virtually identical in its impact to the grace scale used in the present volume). Not only was the "youth" curve of sexual fulfillment in marriage, for example, parallel with religious imagery, but the two also correlated with each other. Indeed, it was possible to account for two-thirds of the rebound in sexual fulfillment in marriage in the last two years of the first decade by a parallel rebound in religious imagery.

In this chapter I propose to push somewhat further in the investigation of these two life cycle phenomena. The first question to ask is whether the religious imagination undergoes the same slump of the mid-twenties as the religious devotion decline. Table 9.1 shows the variation through the years of a religious devotion scale made up of Mass attendance, communion reception, and frequency of prayer. The "z" score is a measure of deviation from mean score on the factors. Thus, a positive "z" score of .31 indicates that teenagers are thirty-one percent of a standard deviation above the mean on their scores on religious devotion.

A comparison of Tables 9.1 and 9.2 indicates that while religious devotion fluctuates during the twenties, the religious imagination does not seem to do so. The alienating life cycle phenomenon of the middle twenties may affect the young person's religious devotion. It does not affect his religious imagination.

TABLE 9.1

Religious Devotion Scale [a] by Cohort
(Z Score High = Devout)

Age	Z Score
18–20	.31
21–23	−.02
24–27	−.13
28–30	−.05

[a] Factor made up of Mass, communion and prayer.

TABLE 9.2

"Grace" Scale by Cohort
(Z Score High = Devout)

Age	Z Score
18–20	.04
21–23	.02
24–27	−.04
28–20	.00

Furthermore, as reported in the previous books, marriage and age lead to a rebound in religious devotion. However, those who are not married in their middle and later twenties are the least devout of all (Table 9.3, page 109). Apparently, neither marriage as such nor aging as such makes any difference in the religious imagination (Table 9.4, page 109). The quality of their religious imagination may be affected by the quality of the spouse's religious imagination—indeed, as we demonstrated in the last chapter, very powerfully affected—but the sheer fact of marriage has no impact whatsoever on the religious imagination. One's stories of God are neither affected by the alienation of the middle twenties nor salvaged by the reintegration which occurs at the end of the middle twenties—a fact which may be very useful for Church leadership to keep in mind when they are dealing with the devotionally and institutionally alienated young people currently in their twenties. Whatever may have happened to their devotional practices and their sexual attitudes, their religious imagination or stories of grace, their pictures of God and Jesus and Mary—with the enormous potential these are capable of having over aspects of their lives—seem utterly unaffected by the middle twenty life cycle.

TABLE 9.3

Devotion by Marital Status by Cohort
(Z Score High = Devout)

Age	Married	Not Married
22–23	.15	−.18
24–27	−.07	−.13
28–30	.07	−.28

TABLE 9.4

Grace Scale by Cohort by Marital Status
(Percent in top quartile on grace scale)

Age	Married	Not Married
21–23	16	21
24–27	17	19
28–30	19	19

The next question to be addressed is whether the life cycle return to religious devotion that we have tentatively identified at the end of the twenties continues in the decade of the thirties. We were able to turn to NORC's *General Social Survey*, looking only at the years 1977 and 1978 to see whether this phenomenon continues or comes to an end in the fourth decade of life. The evidence (Table 9.5, page 110) is quite dramatic. As young Catholics move toward their fortieth birthday, their religious devotion increases substantially. Forty-four percent of those in their early thirties go to church almost every week, as do 60 percent of those in their middle thirties and 70 percent of those in their late thirties. The latter group reached a level of Church devotion parallel to that which was observable in the general Catholic population before the crisis of the late 1960s. Note well that this is not simply a devotion that people presently in their late thirties have always had. It is, rather, a devotion to which they are returning. One need only look at the data reported in *Catholic Schools in a Declining Church* for church attendance of Catholics in their twenties to realize that those Catholics then in their late twenties and now in their early thirties have engaged in a very considerable return to religious devotion.

TABLE 9.5

Church Attendance for Catholics in Their 30's
(Percent)
NORC General Social Survey—(1977–78)

Age Group	Weekly or Almost Weekly
31–33	44
	N = (52)
34–36	60
	N = (48)
37–40	71
	N = (61)

How can one explain this return? Is it marriage? Is it children? Or is it simply the phenomenon of growing older? For those in their thirties on whom we have information from the *General Social Survey* the explanation seems to be aging and not children. The simple "r" between age (from thirty-one to forty) is .1 and the simple "r" for the number of children is .06. When both variables are put into a regression equation the influence of children vanishes and the sheer factor of aging is the only significant correlate with the increase in church attendance.

TABLE 9.6

Correlates With Church Attendance for Catholics in Their 30's

	r	beta
Age	.19	.19
No. of children	.06	.00

For those in their twenties we were able to add to the equation the fact of whether they are married or not. The standardized coefficients (betas) are for age, .34; marriage, .16; and for number of children, 13. Chronological aging, in other words, is as important in explaining the return to religious devotion as the number of children and the fact of marriage put together for Catholic young adults in their twenties.

TABLE 9.7

Correlations with Religious Devotion
(For respondents over 21)

	r	beta
Children	.07	.13
Married	.11	.16
Age	.23	.34

It has frequently been suggested that Catholics who have drifted away from the Church in their twenties will return because of marriage and of child rearing. Both factors play a part during the decade of the twenties when the alienation has been most acute. In the decade of the thirties, however, when most people are married and when many Catholics have completed their child rearing, it is simply the fact of growing older which leads to a "drift" back into the Church. Our data do not enable us to raise the question of whether the age of children has an effect. Perhaps as children begin to ask religious questions there is greater pressure on parents to seek out a more formal and explicit religious identification. However, the mere fact of having children, or having the number of children, one has has no effect at all on the return drift during the thirties.

It may also be that many of those who turned away angrily from the Church in the late 1960s, particularly if they were part of the already institutionally alienated 60s generation, have now found with the passage of time that formal religious devotion (and Catholicism as part of the heritage) is a devotion to which they will return. This may be especially true, one might argue at the present point in this book, because whatever might have happened to their devotion and to their image of the institutional Church, their stories of God, their pictures of Jesus, Mary, God, and heaven—their religious imagination—has been affected neither by life cycle phenomena nor by the crises in the institutional Church. This speculation can certainly be sustained for Catholics under thirty. Further research will be required to be certain that it is true of Catholics over thirty, but the probabilities that it is must be rated as quite high.

The research my colleagues and I reported on in *Catholic Schools in a Declining Church* argued that the reason for the decline in Catholic religious practice between the early 60s and the early 70s was the impact of the birth control encyclical. Without wishing to rehash that argument (which is now largely accepted, in any case), the perspective taken in *Catholic Schools in a Declining Church* leads me to hypothesize that the reason Catholics in their thirties are able to return to religious practice is not that they have become reconciled to the Church's sexual teaching, but that they are more skillful now than in the past at compartmentalizing their devotional Catholicism (and probably their religious imagination) from their sexual ethics. Unfortunately, the *General Social Survey* asks no questions about either birth control or divorce comparable to the ones asked in the two Catholic schools studies, so it is impossible to see if the correlation between church attendance and birth control attitudes and divorce attitudes has degenerated in the last five years. However, there is a surrogate measure in the *General Social Survey* which may be used tentatively to test my speculation—attendance at X-rated movies. Our hypothesis would be that older Catholics would still maintain a fairly close relationship between sexual attitudes and behaviors on the one hand and religious devotion on the other. Whereas the fact that those Catholics in their twenties at the time of the birth control encyclical and now in their thirties have been able to return to religious devotion—precisely because the correlation between sexual behavior and religious devotion has degenerated—indicates a more or less successful compartmentalization of devotion from sexuality. Therefore, we predict a lower correlation between attendance at X-rated movies for Catholics in their thirties as compared to Catholics over forty.

Table 9.8 confirms that expectation. For Catholics over forty the correlation is -.8, for Catholics in their thirties it is -.09. Catholics in their thirties are more likely both to see an occasional X-rated movie and to attend church regularly. For weal or woe, the return to religious devotion and religious identification of Catholics under forty is the result of what seems to be a highly successful compartmentalization of their Catholicism. The alternative, one would suppose, would be a consistent approach which would keep them away from religious stability—a consistency which would doubtless please right-wing Catholics, but which might not so delight Church leadership.

TABLE 9.8

Correlation Between Attendance at X Movies
and Church Attendance for Catholics by Age
(Coefficient of Correlation = Pearson's r)

In thirties	−.09
Over forty	−.18

The next question to be asked in this life cycle chapter is whether the "Kramer vs. Kramer" phenomenon can be found repeating itself in subsequent years of marriage. The *General Social Survey* does, indeed, provide data about marital satisfaction, though we have information from it only about respondents' view of the quality of marriage, and not the respondents' spouses as we did in the cycle report in *The Young Catholic Family*. Furthermore, our measure is a combination of the respondents' estimation of marital satisfaction and family satisfaction. With these two very important considerations in mind we can examine Table 9.9 (page 114), which shows exactly the same decline and rebound in the first ten years of marriage as reported in *The Young Catholic Family*. The rebound remains fairly steady until the twentieth year of the marriage (the decline in the sixteenth and seventeenth years may simply be a result of sampling or it may represent a mini-crisis perhaps accompanying the number of teenagers in the house). However, in the first half of the third decade of the marriage there is another very sharp decline, so that the quality of marital satisfaction is back to where it was in the middle years of the first decade of the marriage. Then, after the twenty-fifth anniversary is over, the marriage rebounds again and the level of satisfaction continues to be moderately high, so that—for those romantics like the present author who are firmly convinced of the need for happy endings to love stories—the score of marital satisfaction between the fifty and fifty-fifth year is the same as it was in the first and second years.

The second and third columns in Table 9.9 depict the scores for men and women and must be viewed very cautiously because the number of cases in each set becomes very small. Generally, however, the pattern is similar between the two sexes, though in the middle of the second decade of the marriage it is the wife who accounts for the mini-slump—perhaps because she has to put up more with the teenagers. However, the major slump in the beginning of the second decade of the marriage occurs in both sexes, as does the rebound after the twenty-fifth anniversary. The decline of women's satisfaction in subsequent years is the result of widowhood, as a wife is much more likely to have lost her spouse after the thirty-fifth year of marriage than a husband is likely to have lost his wife.

The life cycle phenomenon of marital intimacy is not limited to the first decade. There seems to be at least one and possibly more critical turning points thereafter: one in the middle to late teen years of marriage, particularly for a woman (perhaps because of conflicts with teenagers), and then in the first half of the third decade of marriage when both spouses are presumably in their forties and going through the crisis of the middle years (which is, one assumes both physiological and psychological, as well as religious).

Of the two life cycle phenomena, then, one can report that the devotional life cycle crisis of the middle twenties is not affected by the religious imagination, while the marital life cycle phenomenon, at least for those who have been married for less than ten years, is both affected by and affects the religious imagination. Both cycles seem to be relatively benign from the Church's viewpoint. Young people return to the Church in part because they have never lost their Catholic imaginations. Most husbands and wives manage to hang together and come out of their marital slump in the first decade of the marriage certainly because of their religious imagination and in subsequent decades probably because of their religious imagination.

TABLE 9.9

Catholic Married Cycle by Duration of Marriage

(Z Score on factor combining marital satisfaction and family satisfaction)

Years of Marriage	Average Score	Men	Women
1–2	.20	.22	.18
3–4	.05	.15	.02
5–7	.01	.12	.03
8–10	.25	.40	.15
11–15	.26	.11	.37
16–17	−.01	.13	−.12
18–19	.17	.25	.10
20–21	.03	−.07	.10
22–23	.07	.06	.08
25–26	.03	−.07	.10
27–30	.26	.37	.16
30–35	.26	.37	.16
36–40	.10	.20	.00
41–45	.15	.21	.10
45–50	.23	.39	.05
50–55	.20	.42	−.20
56–73	.35	.42	−.20

NOTE: For technical reasons in the data it is only possible to measure the duration of the first marriage. Hence, all who have been divorced are excluded from this table. For this reason, the average score of the table is .19, since the marital happiness for those who have been divorced is much lower than for those who have not been.

TABLE 9.10

Frequent Prayer by Sexual Fulfillment in Marriage by Grace Scale

(Percent of couples in which both spouses pray daily)

Grace Scale	Both Report Fulfillment as "Excellent"	One or Both Not "Excellent"
High	48	23
Low	15	15

The religious imagination is a powerful asset both for the individual and for the Church during life cycle crises. It draws young adults back to religious devotion (though not back to sexual orthodoxy) and it draws husbands and wives back to satisfactory levels of marital intimacy.

Finally (Table 9.10), those couples who are high on the religious image scale are more likely to pray daily than those who are low on the scale. But the difference is statistically significant only if they also report that their sexual fulfillment in marriage is excellent. Indeed, those couples are three times more likely to pray daily than those couples who are sexually fulfilled and lack the religious images, and more than twice as likely to pray daily than those who have the intense images and lack sexual fulfillment. While neither dynamism by itself increases religious devotion appreciably, both together have an immense influence on religious devotion. An earlier chapter established that individual religious devotion is strongly influenced by religious imagination. In this chapter, individuals were being studied; in this final table in Chapter 9 the family unit is analyzed. The joint religious imagination ("your story" and "my story") have become "our story." The correlation between imagination and devotion is very powerful indeed, but only when the joint story of grace ("our story") is reinforced by sexual fulfillment ("our" love affair). The sexual and the religious stories intermingle and interweave in an intricate pattern and have a very powerful effect on religious devotion. Human love combined with a story of grace is linked on a very high level with divine love (as measured by human prayer). St. Paul's religious image about the relationship between the Two Loves is empirically validated.

Doubtless the saint would be pleased to know it, though hardly surprised.

Spiritual Experience and Social Involvement

Highlights

1 A person's social attitudes are reflected in a person's intimately personal religious story and images of God.

2 Persons who picture God as mother and lover are much more likely to be socially concerned than those who do not (Tables 10.1 and 10.2).

3 A concern for social issues is not found to be a result of either membership in particular ethnic groups or regular attendance at church. Images of God were not found to be dramatically different among ethnic groups (Table 10.4).

4 Persons who were socially concerned and who see God as mother and lover were slightly more likely to be otherworldly than those with other images of God (Table 10.5).

5 There is no direct relationship between social concern and any political behaviors such as giving money to candidates, campaigning, or working for causes.

6 Political participation was found to be compatible with spiritual experiences (Table 10.11).

7 Persons' levels of education were positively related to political activities and concern for others.

Chapter 10

Spiritual Experience and Social Involvement

This chapter was prepared by Brother Thomas Hoffman, S.M., on the basis of a classroom presentation he gave in the winter of 1980 at the University of Arizona. Brother Hoffman deserves full credit for thinking of the possible relationships between stories of grace and political commitment and analyzing the nature of the relationship. The technique he uses is somewhat different from the analytic technique which I normally use. But, the direction of his findings is the same as mine. I enthusiastically endorse his work.

The examination of what role, if any, the image one has of God plays with regard to social concern and political behavior is the object of this chapter. If religion has any impact on life in general, in terms of how one conducts oneself with regard to other people and the public sector, it is of paramount importance to look at the content of religion itself; not its content in terms of what doctrinal beliefs one subscribes to, not its content in terms of what generalizations can be made about its traditions, but rather its content in terms of the "pictures in people's heads," their images of God. It is this intimately personal religious story which should have an impact on people's attitudes and behaviors.

The data used in this chapter come from the NORC *Study of Religious Values* conducted in 1979. The nationwide sample consists of Catholics and former Catholics aged 14 to 29.

The hypothesis of independence between specified variables will be tested using either Pearson's chi-square (X^2) or the Likelihood ratio chi-square (L^2). Hierarchical comparisons of various models will be used to examine the structure of religious relationships among variables (see Duncan and Duncan, 1978; Fienberg, 1977; and Goodman, 1978). Likelihood ratio chi-square (L^2) will be used to test the models. Partitioning will be done before collapsing certain variables (see Duncan, 1975). Parameters which describe the structure of relationships will be calculated (see Duncan, 1979). Path analysis will also be used to test hypothesized relationships.

In terms of images of God, I would suspect that those having "warm," loving images of God, such as mother and lover, would be more likely to show social concern than those who hold other images of God. This is based on the notion that if one sees God as a lover or a mother, if one feels loved, one is able to love (see, for example, Jeremiah 29:11–14, 31:3; Hosea 2:21–22; Ezekiel 16:8; Isaiah 62:4–5; John 13:1). One sees God as in love with himself or herself. Mutuality begets fraternity. The image of God as a mother (see, for example, Is. 49:14–15, 66:13) connotes the image of a family, the family of man. Concern for one's brothers should be engendered. If one feels loved, if one has the warmth of a mother, one may have the security, the self-confidence to be able to love and care for others.

The most distinctive group in terms of social concern is made up of those who see God as mother (Tables 10.1 and 10.2, pages 121-122). For those who see God as mother the odds-on yes to social concern are 1.872 times greater than the odds-on yes for those who do not see God as mother. Further, if a person sees God as mother, the odds are 4.162 to 1 that the person will be socially concerned. Other images of God which show significant departure from independence between social concern and image of God are that of lover, redeemer, and judge (a cliffhanger). If a person sees God as lover, the odds are 3.203 to 1 that the person with be socially concerned.

It could be contended that the association between certain images of God and social concern is really a result of ethnic group rather than of image of God. Some ethnic groups have been and are socially dispossessed and therefore may be more concerned with solving problems such as poverty. This is not the case. Social concern and ethnic group are independent (Table 10.3, page 123). Further, there is no dramatic difference in the order of popularity of the images of God among ethnic groups (Table 10.4, page 123).

Perhaps social concern is really a result of church attendance. A person who goes to church more often would possibly be more likely to learn the "golden rule." Also, if church attendance were positively associated with social concern, perhaps it would be positively associated with those means by which social concern can be put into practice: political behavior. Neither of these contentions hold up (Table 10.3). The hypothesis of independence between church attendance and social concern cannot be rejected. For these young Catholics and former Catholics, the null hypothesis cannot be rejected with regard to the hypothesized relationship between church attendance and any of the political behaviors listed (at the .05 level).

TABLE 10.1

Images of God by Social Concern

	SOCIAL CONCERN [b]			
IMAGE OF GOD [a]	Extremely Important	Somewhat Important	Not Too Important	Not Important At All
Judge				
Extremely Likely	133	169	68	12
Somewhat Likely	90	209	118	9
Not Too Likely	68	157	77	22
Not Likely At All	66	91	53	12
Protector				
Extremely Likely	227	350	173	20
Somewhat Likely	92	183	102	23
Not Too Likely	25	61	24	4
Not Likely At All	14	33	21	8
Redeemer				
Extremely Likely	186	276	130	17
Somewhat Likely	96	199	100	17
Not Too Likely	44	93	60	12
Not Likely At All	28	49	29	9
Lover				
Extremely Likely	132	181	79	14
Somewhat Likely	67	126	58	7
Not Too Likely	54	137	60	7
Not Likely At All	104	179	122	27
Master				
Extremely Likely	189	259	129	19
Somewhat Likely	66	166	84	18
Not Too Likely	54	111	50	7
Not Likely At All	50	88	59	11
Mother				
Extremely Likely	64	66	27	4
Somewhat Likely	71	107	37	6
Not Too Likely	82	192	87	7
Not Likely At All	135	258	168	38
Creator				
Extremely Likely	288	465	227	33
Somewhat Likely	50	119	72	16
Not Too Likely	11	27	12	3
Not Likely At All	10	16	11	3
Father				
Extremely Likely	239	382	195	32
Somewhat Likely	64	139	66	8
Not Too Likely	27	62	30	5
Not Likely At All	27	42	29	10

[a] Question wording: "When you think about God, how likely are each of these images to come to your mind?"

[b] Question wording: "Indicate how important each thing is to you. . . . Helping solve social problems such as poverty and air pollution."

TABLE 10.2

Results of Crossclassification of Image of God by Social Concern

Image of God [a]	ODDS Important to Solve Social Problems: Not Important [b]	L²c	p	ODDS RATIO
Judge	2.903	3.18	.05>p>.10	1.246
Protector	2.679	.64(N.S.)	>.40	1.148
Redeemer	2.867	7.812	<.01	1.474
Lover	3.203	9.577	<.01	1.459
Master	2.72	1.025(N.S.)	>.30	1.140
Mother	4.162	19.44	<.001	1.872
Creator	2.649	.605(N.S.)	>.40	1.2005
Father	2.738	2.483(N.S.)	>.10	1.282

[a] Image of God: "When you think about God, how likely are each of these images to come to your mind?" Extremely likely and Somewhat likely = yes; Not too likely and Not likely at all = No.
[b] Social Concern: "Indicate how important each thing is to you. Helping solve social problems such as poverty and air pollution." Very important and somewhat important = important; not too important and not important at all = not important.
[c] The likelihood Ratio — chi-square statistics reported here all refer to 2 by 2 tables with 1 degree of freedom each.

It would seem that those who are most likely to be socially concerned, those who see God as mother or lover, would be those least likely to concentrate on otherworldliness. However, that is not necessarily the case (Table 10.5, page 124). Indeed, those who see God as mother or lover are slightly more likely to be otherworldly than those who have other images of God. It is well to note, however, that for all images of God, the overwhelming response is disagreement with otherworldliness.

As all indications point to the conclusion that the group most socially concerned is made up of those who see God as mother, we shall focus on them to see if this image and social concern have some impact on political behavior. Granted the fact that social concern can be put into practice in a number of ways, it would appear that one of these ways would be through political participation. It would seem that social concern should be positively associated with the various political behaviors. As seeing God as mother appears to be positively associated with social concern, one who sees God as mother should be more likely to participate in the various political activities.

For all the political behaviors, the association between seeing God as mother and social concern holds up (Tables 10.7 and 10.8, page

127) and is included in the preferred models. There is no direct relationship between social concern and voting or attending rallies. There is a direct, positive relationship between social concern and the other four political behaviors (Tables 10.7 and 10.8). However, there is no direct relationship between seeing God as mother and any of the political behaviors. Maybe these people express their social concern in arenas other than the political one.

TABLE 10.3

Pearson Chi-Square Statistics for Various Cross Classifications

	d.f.	x^2	p
Social concern by church attendance	21	13.935	.87
Social concern by ethnic group [a]	18	25.345	.12
Church attendance by vote	7	5.43	.61
Church attendance by contribute money	7	12.959	.07
Church attendance by attend rally	7	4.326	.74
Church attendance by campaign	7	2.403	.94
Church attendance by work for cause	7	6.528	.52
Church attendance by contact official	7	5.784	.57

[a] To which group do you belong? White; Black; Hispanic . . . ; Asian/Pacific Islander; North American Indian, Alaskan native; Other.

TABLE 10.4

Images of God by Ethnic Group
(Percent Extremely Likely and Somewhat Likely)

Image of God	General Population	Order	White	Order	Black	Order	Hispanic	Order
Creator	93.3	1	92.9	1	97.5	1	94.7	1
Protector	86.2	2	80.6	3	89.7	3	89.1	2
Father	82.9	3	81.9	2	94.9	2	88.2	3
Redeemer	76	4	75.8	4	84.2	4	75.6	5
Master	68.4	5	67.5	5	82.1	5	75.8	4
Judge	59.9	6	58.5	6	76.3	6	66.1	6
Lover	49.1	7	48.2	7	69.2	7	47.2	7
Mother	27.9	8	25.3	8	51.2	8	41.9	8

As more parsimonious models were able to be found as a result of both partitioning and testing constrained models (Table 10.8), parameters were able to be calculated (Table 10.9, page 129) which help describe more clearly the relationships existing between social concern, seeing God as mother, and the political behaviors of giving money, campaigning, and working for causes.

TABLE 10.5

Results of Crossclassification of Image of God by Otherwordliness [a]

See God As:	Otherwordly (%)
Judge	8.7
Protector	8.68
Redeemer	9.4
Lover	11.06
Master	10.2
Mother	13.7
Creator	8.37
Father	9.2

[a] For this table one is said to see God in a certain way if the response was either "Extremely Likely" or "Somewhat Likely." The respondent is considered "otherwordly" if she/he agreed or agreed strongly with this statement: "A good Christian ought to think about the next life and not worry about fighting against poverty and injustice in this life."

The parameters $\hat{x} = 1.69$ and $\hat{z} = 1.55$ or 1.59 indicate that for all three behaviors those who are high in seeing God as mother are high in social concern and that those who are low in seeing God as mother are low in social concern. This tendency is somewhat stronger with the high category.

The parameters $\hat{b} = 1.162$ for giving money, 1.511 for campaigning, and 1.562 for working for a cause, indicate that those who are high in social concern are more likely to participate and those who are low in social concern are more likely to refrain from participation. The impact of social concern is somewhat greater with regard to campaigning and working for causes than for giving money. (Perhaps this is because giving money is an easy way to salve one's conscience whereas campaigning and working for causes may require more genuine commitment.)

In much of the professional literature, sex has been shown to have an impact on political behavior (see Milbraith and Goel, 1977:116; Verba, Nie, and Kim, 1978:234). Males have been shown to participate more than women. Interestingly enough, among these young Catholics and former Catholics, after testing models which include items such as seeing God as mother, social concern, and sex, only two of the political behaviors indicate a direct impact of sex on participation: giving money (Table 10.10, page 130) and contacting public officials (preferred models 234, 123, 124).

TABLE 10.6

Social Concern by Likelihood of Seeing God as Mother
by Political Behavior

(3) POLITICAL BEHAVIOR	(2) GOD AS MOTHER	(1) SOCIAL CONCERN			
Vote in Last 3–4 yrs.		Extremely Important	Somewhat Important	Not Too Important	Not Important At All
YES	Extremely Likely	15	24	13	0
	Somewhat Likely	27	37	15	3
	Not Too Likely	32	78	35	5
	Not Likely At All	51	131	83	15
NO	Extremely Likely	21	15	7	1
	Somewhat Likely	14	37	11	1
	Not Too Likely	15	48	25	0
	Not Likely At All	40	74	51	13
Gave Money to Politics in Last 3–4 yrs.					
YES	Extremely Likely	8	14	2	0
	Somewhat Likely	14	20	9	2
	Not Too Likely	13	46	13	1
	Not Likely At All	34	80	40	6
NO	Extremely Likely	28	25	18	1
	Somewhat Likely	27	54	17	2
	Not Too Likely	34	80	46	4
	Not Likely At All	57	126	94	22
Attended Rally/ Meeting in 3–4 yrs.					
YES	Extremely Likely	7	5	4	0
	Somewhat Likely	7	13	1	0
	Not Too Likely	15	26	8	1
	Not Likely At All	23	44	25	5
NO	Extremely Likely	29	33	16	1
	Somewhat Likely	34	61	25	4
	Not Too Likely	32	98	52	4
	Not Likely At All	68	161	109	23

TABLE 10.6—*Continued*

Social Concern by Likelihood of Seeing God as Mother
by Political Behavior

(3) POLITICAL BEHAVIOR	(2) GOD AS MOTHER	(1) SOCIAL CONCERN			
Campaigned in 3−4 yrs.		Extremely Important	Somewhat Important	Not Too Important	Not Important At All
YES	Extremely Likely	5	5	0	0
	Somewhat Likely	6	7	2	0
	Not Too Likely	10	11	5	0
	Not Likely At All	11	20	11	2
NO	Extremely Likely	31	34	21	1
	Somewhat Likely	35	67	24	4
	Not Too Likely	37	115	54	5
	Not Likely At All	80	186	123	26
Worked for Cause in Last 3−4 yrs.					
YES	Extremely Likely	5	3	2	0
	Somewhat Likely	3	8	3	0
	Not Too Likely	13	16	7	0
	Not Likely At All	21	23	13	1
NO	Extremely Likely	31	36	18	1
	Somewhat Likely	38	66	23	4
	Not Too Likely	34	110	52	5
	Not Likely At All	70	183	121	27
Contact Public Official in Last 3−4 yrs.					
YES	Extremely Likely	8	8	0	0
	Somewhat Likely	8	16	2	0
	Not Too Likely	11	27	15	1
	Not Likely At All	25	56	23	3
NO	Extremely Likely	28	31	20	1
	Somewhat Likely	33	58	24	4
	Not Too Likely	36	99	45	4
	Not Likely At All	66	150	111	25

TABLE 10.7

Results of Fitting Alternative Models to
Data Selected From Table 10.5

Models	Marginals Fitted [a]			VOTE d.f.	VOTE L^2	VOTE p	RALLY d.f.	RALLY L^2	RALLY p	CONTACT OFFICIAL d.f.	CONTACT OFFICIAL L^2	CONTACT OFFICIAL p
(1)	1	2	3	24	53.597	<.001	24	50.586	<.01	24	58.944	<.001
(2)	23	1		21	50.394	<.001	21	46.441	<.01	21	55.329	<.001
(3)	13	2		21	53.107	<.001	21	45.190	<.01	21	49.687	<.001
(4)	12	3		15	20.325*	.16	15	17.429*	.29	15	25.785	.04
(5)	12	13		12	19.835	.07	12	12.034	.44	12	16.528*	.17
(6)	23	12		12	17.122	.15	12	13.284	.35	12	22.170	.04
(7)	23	13		18	49.904	<.001	18	41.045	<.01	18	46.073	<.001
(8)	23	12	13	9	16.892	.051	9	6.408	.70	9	11.268	.26

[a] Marginals are identified by variable numbers shown in Table 9.6.
* Preferred Model.

TABLE 10.8

Results of Fitting Alternative Models to Data [a]
Selected From Table 10.5

Model	Marginals [b] and Constraints [c] Fitted			GIVE MONEY d.f.	GIVE MONEY L^2	GIVE MONEY p	CAMPAIGN d.f.	CAMPAIGN L^2	CAMPAIGN p	WORK FOR CAUSE d.f.	WORK FOR CAUSE L^2	WORK FOR CAUSE p
(1)	1	2	3	12	37.503	<.001	12	35.712	<.001	12	44.535	<.001
(2)	23	1		10	34.388	<.001	10	35.366	<.001	10	41.538	<.001
(3)	13	2		10	30.188	<.001	10	28.036	<.01	10	32.712	<.001
(4)	12	3		8	12.863	.12	8	11.072	.20	8	19.895	.011
(5)	12	13		6	5.548	.48	6	3.396	.76	6	8.072	.23
(6)	23	12		6	9.748	.14	6	10.726	.097	6	16.897	<.01
(7)	23	13		8	27.073	<.001	8	27.689	<.001	8	29.715	<.001
(8)	23	12	13	4	1.289	.86	4	3.088	.54	4	3.430	.49
(9)	12_c	13_L		8	11.489*	>.10	8	4.573*	>.80	8	10.353*	>.30

[a] It was found, as a result of partitioning, that for social concern "not too important" and "not important at all" could be combined; and for God as mother "Extremely Likely" and "Somewhat Likely" could be combined. The results reported here are based on these collapsed versions of the variables.
[b] Marginals are identified by variable numbers shown in Table 10.6.
[c] L as a subscript indicates a linear constraint. When the 12 relationship is constrained such as to have x1=x2, y1=y2, z1=z2 it is indicated by the subscript c.
* Preferred model.

Males' odds of saying yes to giving money are 1.563 times greater than the females' odds on yes: 37.39 percent of the males gave money whereas 27.74 percent of the females did so. Only 21.09

percent of the females who were not socially concerned contributed whereas 27.74 percent of the socially concerned females did so. Of the males who were not socially concerned, 32.31 percent gave money while 39.54 percent of the males who were socially concerned contributed. This helps to illustrate that both social concern and sex influenced campaign contributions.

People who are socially concerned are more likely to contact public officials. Males are more likely than females to contact officials—24.71 percent of the males contacted a public official (22.9 percent if not socially concerned and 25.49 percent if concerned); 18.96 percent of the females contacted a public official (9.52 percent if not socially concerned and 22.88 percent of socially concerned).

One might suspect that having spiritual experiences would lead a person to have less concern with such mundane matters as political participation. However, with regard to attending rallies (preferred models 234, 134, 12), campaigning, working for causes, and contacting public officials (Table 10.11, page 131) quite the reverse is the case.

Of those who have had one or more spiritual experiences, 25.06 percent attended political rallies, while only 15.6 percent of those who have not went. Further, in terms of the effects of having a spiritual experience on campaigning, working for a cause, and contacting a public official, the odds of having participated are, respectively, 2.232, 2.053, and 2.223 times greater for those who have had a spiritual experience than the odds on having participated for those who haven't had such an experience. Rather than going for "pie in the sky by and by," those with spiritual experience(s) come down "from the mountaintop," so to speak, to go out and participate in the political process.

Thus far it has been observed that certain images of God (particularly mother and lover) are positively associated with social concern. Further, the observation has been made that social concern is positively related to four out of six political activities. Positive association has been established between spiritual experience and political participation. Sex has a direct impact on only two of the political behaviors. No direct association has been established between seeing God as mother and political participation.

Up to now a single item indicator has been used to measure social concern. After factor analysis, in which numerous indicators of what one holds to be important and what role oneself and/or the Church should play with regard to various issues of justice, a variable was constructed (Figure 10.1, page 132) which will be called "Social Concern."[1]

TABLE 10.9

**Fitted Counts and Parameter Estimates under Model 9
for Give Money, Campaign, Work for Cause**

Political Behavior	See God as Mother	Fitted Counts — Social Concern			Parameter Estimates		
		Extremely Important	Somewhat Important	Not Too Important & Not Important At All			
Give Money							
YES	Extremely Likely & Somewhat Likely	27.54	35.45	15.94	1.959	1	1
	Not Too Likely	18.08	40.83	17.65	1.162	1.04	1
	Not Likely At All	31.28	67.90	47.32	1.162	1	1.549
NO	Extremely Likely & Somewhat Likely	49.46	73.97	38.64	1.687	1	1.162
	Not Too Likely	32.47	85.17	42.78	1	1.04	1.162
	Not Likely At All	56.17	141.66	114.68	1	1	1.801
Campaign							
YES	Extremely Likely & Somewhat Likely	11.14	11.02	3.77	2.546	1	1
	Not Too Likely	7.31	12.68	4.17	1.5105	1.04	1
	Not Likely At All	12.64	21.10	11.18	1.5105	1	1.586
NO	Extremely Likely & Somewhat Likely	65.86	98.41	50.81	1.686	1	1.511
	Not Too Likely	43.25	113.31	56.27	1	1.04	1.511
	Not Likely At All	74.79	188.46	150.83	1	1	2.395
Work for Cause							
YES	Extremely Likely & Somewhat Likely	14.04	13.67	4.57	2.634	1	1
	Not Too Likely	9.22	15.74	5.06	1.562	1.04	1
	Not Likely At All	15.94	26.18	13.57	1.562	1	1.55
NO	Extremely Likely & Somewhat Likely	62.96	95.75	50.00	1.686	1	1.562
	Not Too Likely	41.34	110.25	55.37	1	1.04	1.562
	Not Likely At All	71.50	183.38	148.43	1	1	2.421
					bx	1	1
					b	y	1
					b	1	z
					x	1	b
					1	y	b
					1	1	bz

Another variable that was constructed was God as mother/lover. Although much of what has been discussed so far implied that this could be seen as a single variable, factor analysis gave a firm foundation for this construction.

TABLE 10.10

Observed and Fitted Counts for Contribute Money by Social Concern, God as Mother, and Sex

(4) Sex	(3) God as Mother [a]	(2) Social Concern [b]	(1) Gave Money Observed		Fitted [c]	
			Yes	No	Yes	No
Male	Yes	Yes	25	55	32.10	47.90
		No	6	16	6.81	15.19
	No	Yes	96	130	90.67	135.33
		No	36	72	33.42	74.57
Female	Yes	Yes	31	79	33.01	76.99
		No	7	22	6.46	22.54
	No	Yes	71	167	73.22	170.78
		No	24	94	26.30	91.70

Odds Ratio
For 14 Association: 1.563

[a] See note 1 Table 10.2.
[b] See note 2 Table 10.2.
[c] Marginal Fitted: 234 12 14; d.f. = 5, L^2 = 4.421, p = .49.

In order to examine in detail the impact various images, attitudes, experiences, and characteristics have on political participation, the various behaviors have been examined individually. However, in order to examine how politically active a person may be, one can add up the number of behaviors the respondent participates in to create a variable that will be called "Political Activities."

One very important variable not yet discussed which has been shown by a number of researchers to have an impact on political participation is education (see Milbraith and Goel, 1977:98–102). This research has indicated a positive relationship between political participation and education.

Given previous research, education should be positively related to political activities. Further, common sense would indicate that education is positively associated with concern for others (as operationalized here) since support for integration, poverty programs, and so forth, appears to come from the more highly educated sector of society. Education would probably be negatively related to spiritual experience since, in this "secular" society, education purports to bring people "beyond" such things. Education should probably also be related in a positive manner to God as mother/lover since these are images which result in social concern, and since these also appear to be somewhat less than mainstream images.

TABLE 10.11

Observed and Fitted Counts for Campaign, Work for Cause, and Contact Public Official by Social Concern, God as Mother, and Experience of Spirit

Spirit [a]	God as Mother [b]	Social Concern [c]	Campaign Observed		Campaign Fitted [d]		Work for Cause Observed		Work for Cause Fitted		Contact Public Official Observed		Contact Public Official Fitted	
			Yes	No	Yes	No	Yes	No	Yes	No	Yes	No	Yes	No
Yes	Yes	Yes	13	78	14.38	76.62	13	78	12.74	78.26	21	70	25.63	65.37
		No	1	16	1.82	15.18	3	14	1.59	15.41	2	15	1.04	15.96
	No	Yes	30	168	31.29	166.71	41	157	40.93	157.07	68	130	66.89	131.11
		No	13	76	9.52	79.48	11	79	12.75	77.25	26	64	23.44	66.56
No	Yes	Yes	9	87	7.45	88.55	5	91	7.05	88.95	19	77	14.37	81.63
		No	1	33	1.73	32.27	2	32	1.62	32.38	0	34	.96	33.04
	No	Yes	22	247	20.88	248.12	32	237	30.29	238.71	49	220	50.11	218.89
		No	5	131	6.93	129.07	10	125	10.04	124.96	16	120	18.56	117.44
Odds Ratio for 14 Association			2.232				2.053				2.223			

[a] Spirit: "How often in your life have you had an experience where you felt as though you were very close to a powerful, spiritual force that seemed to lift you out of yourself?" Once or twice, several times, often = Yes (those who have definitely had such an experience). Never in my life, I cannot answer this question = No.
[b] See note 1 Table 10.2.
[c] See note 2 Table 10.2.

[d] Behavior	Marginals			Fitted	d.f.	L²	P
Campaign	234	12		14	5	3.406	.64
Cause	234	12	13	14	4	2.326	.68
Contact	234	123		14	3	6.407	.093

Although our initial suspicion was that spiritual experiences would be negatively related to political participation, that suspicion was wrong. Thus, spiritual experience should be positively related to political participation. Since, in recent years, it has appeared (at least through media presentation) that politics based on religious principles has been conservatively-oriented, it would seem that spiritual experience should be negatively related to concern for others and God as mother/lover.

We have already seen that certain images of God have been positively associated with social concern and that social concern has been positively associated with certain political behaviors.

Thus, we would expect God as mother/lover to be positively associated with concern for others, and concern for others to be positively associated with political activities.

FIGURE 10.1

Path Analysis of Variables [1]
Contributing to Political Activities

Standardized and Unstandardized (within parentheses)
Regression Coefficients

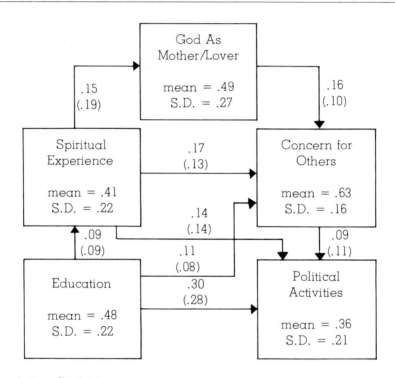

Correlation Coefficients

	POL	CONCERN	SPIR	GODML
CONCERN	.14			
SPIR	.18	.20		
GODML	−.03*	.18	.14	
EDUC	.32	.12	.09	−.02*

* Not significant

[1] "Political Activities" refers to the number of political activities (all discussed earlier—see Table 10.6) a person has participated in.

After examining the results of a principal component factor analysis with varimax rotation, the "God as Mother/Lover" variable was constructed by combining responses picturing God as "Mother" and God as "Lover."

After examining the results of a maximum Likelihood factor analysis with verimax rotation, the "Concern" variable was constructed by adding responses to "Social Concern" (See note 2, Table 10.1 for wording), "Social Action" (How important is it to "involve the Church more in social action, for example, promoting integration of human rights."), "End Segregation" (Level of agreement with this statement: "There is an obligation to work for the end of racial segregation."), "Aid poor" ("Even though a person has a hard time making ends meet, he should still try to give some of his money to help the poor."), and "Self-knowledge" (How important is: "spending a lot of time getting to know your inner self.").

Some of these speculations are supported, and some of them can be refuted (Figure 10.1).

Education, as expected, is positively related to political activities and concern for others. However, there is no relationship between it and God as mother/lover. Also, contrary to expectation, it is positively related to spiritual experience. What does this tell us? First, it indicates that education does not help nor hurt anyone in terms of having a warm image of God. Further, it indicates that perhaps education may help open one up to further experiences rather than close one off from them. (It could be contended that in certain religious traditions one is expected to have some sort of religious experience: of "receiving Christ into one's heart" or of "getting the spirit," and thus these experiences are no more than self-fulfilled prophesies. However, one should recall that this sample consists of young people who are or were members of the Catholic Church, a religion that does not have such expectations.)

Spiritual experience is positively related to political activities. Further, rather than being negatively related to seeing God as mother/lover and negatively related to concern for others, it is positively related to both. Those who have had spiritual experience are more likely to have a warm image of God. Perhaps it is this intimate, personal experience which allows one to see God as an intimate, loving, caring being. Spiritual experience is also positively related to concern for others. Perhaps, since there has been an experience of something beyond the mundane, something beyond this "petty pace," one is able to see beyond oneself to the larger world out there. Further, seeing God as mother/lover is positively related to concern for others. If one feels loved, if one has experienced graciousness, one is able to be concerned for others. And one of the ways, certainly not the only way, that this concern can be actualized is through political activity, which the positive relationship between concern for others and political activities indicates is indeed the case.

To sum up, an active citizenry should be educated. The end result of education, however, will be an active citizenry which has spiritual experiences (and thus warmer images of God) and concern for others. It is possible that the issues which would be raised in the public forum would be more and more rooted in a humane ethic based upon a foundation of spiritual experience and buttressed by warm images of God. Education, rather than secularizing, may indeed be humanizing and spiritualizing.

NOTES

[1]Interestingly enough, a concern for setting aside enough time to know oneself clustered with these other variables. Perhaps it is through following that ancient maxim, "know thyself," that one finds there exists an essential unity among all humans. This recognition would engender a greater concern for others.

Teenagers: Toward a New Religious Consciousness?

Highlights

1 *There is some evidence to indicate that young Catholics (thirteen to seventeen years of age) may represent a new religious consciousness which could have enormous importance for the future of Catholicism.*

2 *Adolescents in the United States and English Canada differed significantly from young adults in their attitudes toward God as lover and mother, and heaven as a place of intense pleasure and action. French-Canadian teenagers, however, are not different from young adults in these areas. American and English-Canadian teenagers are moving toward an image of God as mother and lover. They are catching up to the way in which the French-Canadian teenagers tend to picture God today (Tables 11.1, 11.2).*

3 *The parish seems to have been a positive vehicle in communicating and sustaining the new religious consciousness. The more a young adult is linked to the Church through the parish, the stronger the correlation in religious attitudes between the two age groups.*

4 *The majority of Catholic teenagers want to see an updating of Catholic sexual teachings; improvement in the quality of sermons; improvements in the quality of Church leadership (Table 11.18).*

5 *Catholic teenagers are also considerably more devout in their religious behavior than young adults. There is a strong correlation between their religious attitudes and their religious devotion. This makes today's teenagers excellent prospects for religious vocations (Table 11.9).*

6 *Socialization in religious imagery occurs in relationships rather than in formal education situations. In the case of today's young Catholics it has been transmitted through devout mothers and/or sympathetic priests.*

Chapter 11

Teenagers: Toward a New Religious Consciousness?

Teenagers, it has always been argued, are *different*. Sometimes this is a compliment; sometimes it is a criticism. Normally both the compliment and the criticism are abandoned with the passage of time as adolescents become young adults and leave their teenage diversity behind. The Catholic adolescents of the United States and Canada studied by the NORC team are indeed different, sometimes strikingly so, in their religious attitudes and behaviors from those young adults from age eighteen to thirty. The younger Catholics—thirteen to seventeen years of age—may not display the same teenage rebellion as those who preceded them. There is some reason to believe that they represent a new religious consciousness, a shift in the way of thinking about God and the purpose of human life which could have enormous importance for the future of Catholicism.

Adolescents in the United States (Table 11.1, page 138) are 16 percentage points more likely than young adults to think of God as a lover, 11 percentage points more likely to think of God as a mother, 12 percentage points more likely to think of heaven as a life like the one here on earth only better, 12 percentage points more likely to think of heaven as a life of intense action, and 19 percentage points more likely to think of heaven as a paradise of pleasure and delight. A parallel difference between adolescents and young adults can be found in English Canada. French-Canadian teenagers, however, are not different from young adults, either in their image of God as a lover or as mother, or their picture of heaven as a life of intense action. It seems that both English-Canadian and American young people are moving toward the image of God as lover and mother. They are catching up to a more tender and affectionate French-Canadian "story" of God.

In the United States, the teenagers are approximately 20 percentage points higher than young adults on each of the scales.

The same phenomenon can be observed among the English Canadians. While there is no change in the God scale among French-Canadian young people, they are 13 percentage points higher on the heaven-as-action-paradise scale than the young adults and 9 percentage points higher on the religious consciousness scale.

TABLE 11.1

Post-Vatican Religious Consciousness in the United States and Canada

(Percent)

	UNITED STATES		ENGLISH CANADA		FRENCH CANADA	
	Adoles-cents [a]	Adults	Adoles-cents [a]	Adults	Adoles-cents [a]	Adults
God as lover [b]	60	44	68	51	90	90 [c]
God as Mother	36	25	40	22	45	39 [c]
Heaven as:						
a life like the one here only better	70	58	73	52	56	45
a life of intense action	35	27	44	28	22	23 [c]
a paradise of pleasures and delights	72	53	71	46	70	50

[a] Adolescents are 13–71, young adults are 18–30.
[b] Extremely likely or somewhat likely.
[c] Not significant, all other differences in table are significant.

TABLE 11.2

Summary Measures of New Religious Consciousness in the United States and Canada

(Percent)

	UNITED STATES		ENGLISH CANADA		FRENCH CANADA	
	Adoles-cents [a]	Adults	Adoles-cents [a]	Adults	Adoles-cents [a]	Adults
God as mother and lover	63	45	39	25	64	64 [a]
Heaven as action paradise	67	45	66	44	52	39
New image of God and heaven [b]	45	23	35	11	35	26

[a] Not significant; all other differences in table are statistically significant.
[b] Combination of heaven and God images.

The new religious consciousness is somewhat stronger among the adolescent women in the United States than it is among adolescent men (49 percent versus 40 percent on the God/heaven scale) and in English Canada (31 percent for the men and 42 percent for the women). In French Canada, however, the opposite seems to be the case. The teenage men are higher than their women counterparts (and as high as English-Canadian women, higher than English-Canadian men, and higher than American men) on the new religious consciousness (God/heaven) scale. In all three cultures, however, the increase occurred both among young men and among young women. While the new religious consciousness is somewhat stronger among young men than among young women, it is still quite strong among young women (Tables 11.3—11.5).

TABLE 11.3

New Religious Consciousness by Sex (in U.S.)
(Percent)

	MALES		FEMALES	
	Adoles-cents	Adults	Adoles-cents	Adults
God	59	44	67	46
Heaven	65	46	69	44
God/Heaven	40	23	49	23

TABLE 11.4

New Religious Consciousness by Sex (in English Canada)
(Percent)

	MALES		FEMALES	
	Adoles-cents	Adults	Adoles-cents	Adults
God	34	23*	43	27
Heaven	54	42	79	40
God/Heaven	31	13	42	8

* Not significant; all other differences in table are statistically significant.

There are two general explanations that might be applied to the striking difference in religious imagination between teenagers and young adults. The difference may be a "life cycle" phenomenon. A tender, affectionate "story" of God and heaven may be typical of the romantic teen years. Perhaps it will be shattered as soon as the adolescents "grow up" and settle down to the ordinary routines of adult life. The second possible explanation can be found in the "cohort" model. According to such an approach, the religious consciousness found among adolescents is not a phenomenon which will wane but one which will persist throughout life because they are the product of new religious experience and a changing religious culture—in all likelihood, one created by the enormous changes in Catholicism since the Second Vatican Council.

TABLE 11.5

New Religious Consciousness by Sex (in French Canada)
(Percent)

	MALES		FEMALES	
	Adoles- cents	Adults	Adoles- cents	Adults
God	64	59*	65	69*
Heaven	61	45	48	35
God/Heaven	42	31*	31	23*

* Not significant.

One cannot with absolute confidence choose between the two until one returns to the present adolescents to see what has happened to their religious imagination. However, a number of attempts to sustain a life cycle explanation were not successful and two tests which might incline one to a cohort explanation were successful. We are then in the position to conclude, at least tentatively, that the teenagers, all of whom were born after the Council had begun and most of whom came into the world after it ended, do indeed reflect the enormous change in Catholicism since the Council.

Their brighter picture of God and of heaven can *not* be explained as the result of a lower alienation score than young adults nor as the result of lower scores of political radicalism. They do not have a new religious consciousness because they have yet to go through the alienation experience of the middle twenties, nor because they escaped the politically-radicalizing experiences of Vietnam or Watergate, nor can they be said to be more permissive in attitudes towards God because of greater sexual permissiveness or freer use of marijuana, nor is their enthusiasm the result of the growing influence of the charismatic movement. There are no significant correlations, for example, between the new consciousness scale and organizational alienation, political radicalism, the use of drugs, participation in charismatic meetings, yoga, est, a psychoanalytic experience, an encounter group, or any other such self-help, nor is there any connection between it and any form of Catholic education. Nor is it the effect of greater "high spirits" among adolescents as measured by a psychological well-being scale, nor of a higher level of intense religious experience which seems to be more common in adolescents.

Thus, none of the explanations which one might expect to apply to a life cycle model can be sustained by the data. This does not prove the life cycle model wrong; it merely leaves it unproven. But if a more intense, more affectionate, more tender "story" of God which seems to exist in the imagination of many teenagers is not the result of formal education, one would expect that it has been transmitted to young people some way or other by informal socialization mechanisms in the Church—presumably the family and the local parish. If the parish is the instrument of such post-Vatican socialization, then one would predict that those young adults who are closely tied into the parish network would be similar to the teenagers in their religious imagination. Table 11.6 seems to confirm this expectation. There is no statistical difference between adolescents and young adults who are both active in a parish organization and have had a serious religious conversation with a priest during the past year. The difference between adolescents and young adults who have done one or the other of these "parish contact" activities is 14 percentage points (significant at the .05 level), while the difference between the adolescents and young adults who engaged in neither parish-related activity is 25 percentage points (significant in excess of the .001 level). In other words, the more likely a young adult is to be linked to the Church communication network as this network operates in the local parish, the more likely is he or she to share in the post-Vatican religious consciousness. The parish clergy in a mostly informal setting seem to have been able to communicate or sustain the new religious consciousness in young adults.

TABLE 11.6

God/Heaven Scale by Conversation with a Priest and
Sympathy with Pastoral Problems by Parish Priest
(Percent high on Scale)

	Adolescent	Young Adult
Parish priest 'Very understanding" (Yes):		
Conversation with priest—Yes	47	52*
No	59	22
Parish priest "Very understanding" (No):		
Conversation with priest—Yes	46	23
No	43	22

* Not significant.

The influence of the priest in bringing the young adult up to the level of the teenager on the God/heaven scale can be observed in Table 11.6 in which the effect of saying that the parish priest is very understanding and having a conversation with the priest in the past year can be measured. There is no significant variation in the teenage column (the left-hand) as these two influences are considered. Furthermore, in the right-hand column three of the four figures are 22 percent—not significantly different from the adolescent level. However, those young adults who say that the parish priest is very understanding and that they have had a serious conversation with the priest about religion in the last year are likely to score more than twice as high on the God/heaven scale than other young adults (52 percent) and are not significantly different from teenagers. Those young adults who have had a serious conversation with a priest and report that their parish priest is very sympathetic (in all likelihood, the same priest is involved) have similar "stories of God" as do teenagers. It would appear then that we are indeed dealing with a cohort phenomenon with the impact of a major institutional shift—the Vatican Council—which has deeply affected those young people born since the Council and also affects the slightly older group of young adults insofar as they are plugged into the communication network which disseminates religious change.

But how does the consciousness arise in the teenagers? As we can see in the first row of Table 11.7 (page 143), there is no variation among adolescents on the parish contact scale. The only other socialization institution which might be responsible for the new religious consciousness is the family. There were no relationships between the paternal variable and the God/heaven scale but there was a hint of an explanation when one considers mother's education and mother's religious devotion. Young adults had a 23 percent score on the God/heaven scale; teenagers whose mother's education was low and who received communion less than several times a month were 33 percent on the scale. If the mother was a high school graduate who received communion less than several times a month the score went to 40 percent. However, those adolescents whose mothers were frequent communicants, regardless of education, scored 50 percent on the new religious consciousness measure.

It is precisely those teenagers who come from families where there is a devout mother that are likely to be strikingly different in their "faith" of God and heaven in comparison with the young adults (who are not affected at all by their mother's religious devotion in their stories of God). The absence of religious devotion and the mother's education does have some effect on the "story" that lurks in the religious imagination of teenagers.

It seems reasonable to assume that the mothers of today's teenagers were in their twenties or very early thirties during the years of the Vatican Council and hence were especially susceptible. This is particularly true if they were either devout or well educated to the changes in the Church, especially to the results of the Council (obviously quite unintended by the Council fathers) which led to a major reshaping of popular Catholic thinking about the role of women and the nature of human sexuality. It would appear that these devout young mothers were remarkably affected, transmitting what they thought was the meaning of the post-conciliar Church to their children and that they are substantially responsible for the "new religious consciousness" or the "new stories" of God that exist in the imagination of contemporary Catholic adolescents.

TABLE 11.7

New Religious Consciousness and Mother's Education and Reception of Communion
(Percent high on God/Heaven Scale)

All Young Adults	23
Adolescents	
Mothers less than high school grads and less than several times a month communion	33
Mothers high on education, low on communion	40
Mothers high on communion, low on education	50
Mothers high on both communion and education	49

Our contention that adolescents have been socialized into the new religious consciousness by devout mothers, probably devout younger mothers (the educational measure could well in fact be of usefulness, since the younger mothers are better-educated than older mothers) were in the formative period of their religious life during the conciliar years and socialized their own children into the religious consciousness they perceived as emerging from the Council. We also contend that those who were too old to be influenced by their mothers still absorbed the Council through the influence of a sympathetic parish priest with whom they are in close contact.

These arguments are made on the basis of questions such as mother's education, mother's reception of communion, the young person's evaluation of his or her parish priest, and the young person's report of his or her contact with a priest. They do not ask the young person whether he or she perceives a strong influence from the mother or from the parish community.

However, an explicit question about mother's influence enables us to inquire whether these influences, which we have argued have been working on the lives of young people, are perhaps perceived by young people as having an influence on them. One would expect, if the reasoning in this chapter is correct, that precisely those adolescents who report a strong mother influence would be the highest on the God/heaven scale and that perception of those young adults who report a strong parish community influence would be the highest of their group on the God/heaven scale and would not be substantially different from teenagers on this scale. Both these expectations are supported. The only adolescents with high scores on the God/heaven scale are those who report that their mother did indeed have strong religious influence on them (52 percent of those in this category are high on the God/heaven scale). The only young adults who are distinctive on the scale are precisely those who report a strong parish influence on their life (35 percent of them not significantly different from 38 percent of the teenagers reporting the same community influence).

Thus both by objective and subjective measures we are in a position to say that teenagers have been socialized into the new religious consciousness by devout mothers, and young adults into it by sympathetic parish priests. The teenagers did not need parish priests because the mothers had already done the job. The young adults, having escaped the mother's influence, have been socialized by a sympathetic parish priest—if they were fortunate enough to come in contact with one. How do you implement an Ecumenical Council? Through devout mothers and sympathetic priests, of course. How else?

Teenagers also have a somewhat different prayer style than young adults. They are more likely to have high scores on measures that emphasize formal regular prayer said on their knees to specific persons. It is precisely those adolescents who are high on the God/heaven scale who are also the most likely to engage in formal prayer as opposed to informal (Table 11.10A, page 147). Two-thirds of them indeed pray informally using their own words, only slightly less than the young adults. But those who are high on the God/heaven scale are three times as likely to say formal prayers as the young adults who are high on that scale and twice as likely to say formal prayers as adolescents who are low on the God/heaven scale.

This finding at first seems contradictory. How can young people who see God as a mother and a lover and heaven as an action-filled life of pleasure and delight permit themselves to be disciplined by the "rigidities" of formal prayer? Perhaps they do not consider formal prayer rigid and perhaps if their "stories" of God involve such intense and tender loving relationship, they believe in the need of some order, punctuality, and regularity in sustaining that relationship.

The probability then seems tilt in the direction of an authentic cohort phenomenon and one of considerable importance for the Church. The Vatican Council seems to have had a very substantial impact on Catholic teens, an impact that was filtered through their mothers.

What then is this new breed of Catholic teenagers like? They want to see an updating of the Catholic sexual teachings, improvement in the quality of sermons, and in the quality of Church leaders—all in substantial majorities (Table 11.8). A minority that approaches one-half also thinks that it is important that priests be allowed to marry and that women should be ordained (44 percent also favor more order and discipline in the Church). On three issues—order and discipline, marriage of priests, and the updating of sexual ethics—the adolescents are somewhat more conservative than the young adults, although almost 75 percent favor the updating of the Church's sexual teaching, 50 percent support the right of priests to marry.

TABLE 11.8

The Agenda of Adolescents

(Percent)

Changes in the Church	Adolescents	Young Adults
Improve the quality of sermons	70	73
Impose more order and discipline	44	32*
Improve the quality of Church leaders	64	70
Allow priests to marry	49*	55
Allow women to become priests	46	43
Bring the church's teaching on divorce and birth control more in line with current social practices	73*	82
Improvement scale (first three variables)	55	52
Sexuality scale (second three variables)	46*	53

* Significant difference.

Is it possible to advocate order and discipline and still, for example, support the ordination of women and priestly marriage? In many newspaper accounts it would appear that order and discipline is a conservative stance and women and married priests is a liberal stance. If you are a teenager it is not at all inconsistent, it would seem, to be for order and also to be for innovation: 48 percent of those teens who think that order and discipline is important also think that it is important that women be ordained priests, and 51 percent of those who think that order and discipline are extremely important also think it is important that priests be permitted to marry. Those who think that order is extremely important, in other words, are somewhat more likely than those who do not think it is extremely important to support the ordination of women and the marriage of the clergy. Their support of order and discipline is not to be construed as a "conservative" ecclesiastical position.

Their life goals, however, are substantially more liberal (Table 11.9). They are significantly less likely than young adults to consider that a high paying job is "very important" and more likely to consider as "very important" a life goal of "helping to solve social problems such as poverty and air pollution." Also, they are twice as likely (13 percent versus 6 percent) to consider as a very important life goal serving God in a Church career, which could suggest considerable vocation potential among the contemporary teenagers (45 percent of them say that serving God in a Church career is either very important or somewhat important as opposed to 21 percent of the young adults).

TABLE 11.9

Important Life Goals for Adolescents
(Percent very important)

	Adolescents	Young Adults
A high paying job	18	26
Helping to solve social problems such as poverty and air pollution	36	21
Serving God in a Church career	13 (45*)	6 (21*)

* Very important and somewhat important.

They are also considerably more devout in their personal religious behavior than young adults: 68 percent of them go to Mass almost every week (Table 11.10, page 147) as compared to 37 percent of the young adults and more than half of them receive communion every week as opposed to less than one-quarter of young adults. Furthermore, their greater devotion and their greater social commitment are in part the effect of their more tender, passionate, and affectionate religious imagination (Table 11.12, page 148). There is, for adolescents, a significant correlation between their image of God as a lover and mother and frequent church attendance, frequent communion reception, the rejection of money as a life goal, the endorsement of social commitment as a life goal, and a demand for the improvement of the quality of the Church (better sermons, better leadership, better order). There is a very strong .28 correlation between the God as lover/mother and the importance of a career in the Church, suggesting that it is precisely the transformation in religious consciousness that makes today's teenager an especially well-predisposed target for vocational recruiting.

TABLE 11.10

Religious Devotion of Adolescents
(Percent)

	Adolescents	Young Adults
Almost weekly Mass	68	37
Almost weekly communion	55	23

TABLE 11.10A

Prayer Habits by God/Heaven Scale
(Percent "Often pray like this")

		Adolescents	Young Adults
Say Formal Prayers			
God/Heaven Scale:	High	46*	17
	Low	21	20
Use Own Words			
God/Heaven Scale:	High	67	72
	Low	67	77

* Significantly different from both young adults and from adolescents low on the God/Heaven Scale.

TABLE 11.11

Correlations Between Image of God as Lover and Mother and Certain Other Variables for Adolescents Only
(Coefficient of Correlation = Pearson's r)

Church attendance	.16
Communion reception	.09
Importance of money	−.17
Importance of social commitment	.12
Importance of career in church	.28
Improvement of quality of Church scale	.14
Change of sexuality scale	.07*

* Not significant.

Indeed (Table 11.12), it is precisely those who are high in the God as mother/lover measure who are significantly more likely to support the updating of sexual teaching, the ordination of women, and the improvement of sermons. Products of a changing era in the Church, those with the new religious consciousness seem strongly committed to endorsing even more religious change.

TABLE 11.12

Image of God and Changes in the Church
(Percent somewhat important or very important)

	Adolescents		Young Adults	
	High	Low	High	Low
God as Lover/Mother				
Update sexual teachings	78*	72	81	83
Ordain women	49*	43	42	44
Improve sermons	73*	60	77*	68

* Statistically significant.

Will they go through the same "U-curve" in their life of religious devotion that has affected the young adults (which we have described in an earlier chapter)? Will the institutional alienation which today affects unmarried young adults in their middle-twenties also affect today's new breed when they reach the same age?

One has no way of knowing the answer to this question. If the forces at work in our culture making for institutional alienation are still operating, they will come into conflict with the more tender and affectionate story of God in their religious imagination. In the present generation of young adults, those who are high on the God/heaven scale are more likely than those who are low to be devout during the religious crisis of the middle-twenties, but their devotion goes through a curve just the same, with the hope that a decline in religious devotion is not as sharp. It is possible to simulate the next twelve to sixteen years in the lives of today's adolescents by making two assumptions:

1. That the devotion of those on the God/heaven scale remains constant.

2. That at each phase of the cycle the rates of church attendance and communion reception for those who are both high and low on the God/heaven scale will be operative for the adolescents as they move through the cycle.

The result (Table 11.13, page 149) of this simulation showed that there will continue to be (given a continued alienation phenomenon in American culture for those in their middle-twenties) a mini-life cycle in which religious devotion declines. However, the cycle will not be quite so precipitous in the end result as today's teenagers approach their thirtieth birthday. There will be somewhat higher levels of religious devotion than can be found among those who are today approaching their thirtieth birthday. Thirty-two percent of those between twenty-eight and thirty go to church nearly every week now and 21 percent of them receive communion nearly every week. In the simulated model, today's adolescents will, as they approach their thirtieth birthday, be approximately 40 percent in their weekly church attendance and approximately 30 percent in their weekly communion reception—an improvement of about one-quarter in Mass attendance and more than one-third in communion reception.

TABLE 11.13

Projected Religious Life Cycle to Age 30 for Today's Adolescents
(Assuming They Maintain Present Scores on God/Heaven Scale and Attend Mass and Receive Communion at Same Rates for Those Having Comparable Scores at Older Ages)

	PERCENT MASS ALMOST EVERY WEEK		PERCENT COMMUNION ALMOST EVERY WEEK	
	Actual attendance of age cohorts at present	Projected attendance of adolescents during next 12 years	Actual attendance of age cohorts at present	Projected attendance of adolescents during next 12 years
13–17	67	67	54	54
18–22	49	49	32	33
23–27	29	33	17	19
28–30	32	39	21	29

If alienating factors are no worse in our society and if the adolescents cling to their present "story" of God, then the next decade will not be so severe for the Church in the "loss" of young adults. If the alienation factors should grow worse and the religious consciousness fade, then it will be more severe. If the alienation phenomenon fades, then the religious devotion of those in their twenties between now and 1990 will be even higher than the model projects.

We have stressed in this chapter that socialization in religious imagery occurs in relationships rather than in formal education situations. The new, presumably post-conciliar, religious consciousness has been transmitted to young people in their teenage years by devout mothers and, if they are young adults, by sympathetic parish priests. The third great socializing influence we know from previous chapters is the spouse and one may come to passionate love of God as that love is revealed through a spouse quite independently of major shifts in ecclesiastical emphasis. Indeed (Table 11.14), correlation between husbands and wives, both on the God as mother/lover scale and on the God/heaven scale, increases with duration of marriage so that the correlation between spouses on whether God is a mother/lover is .49 by the end of the first decade of marriage and .28 between the spouses on the combined scale of knowing the story of a tender, loving God and an action-filled, pleasurable life in heaven.

TABLE 11.14

**Correlations Between Spouses
by Duration of Marriage**

(Coefficient of Correlation = Pearson's r)

	God as Mother/Lover	God/Heaven
1–2 years	.18	.13*
3–8 years	.30	.13
9–10 years	.49	.28

* Relationship not significant.

Furthermore (Table 11.15), it is in pleasing and sexually-fulfilling marriages that the correlations are strongest (.49 between the two spouses on the God scale and .32 on the God/heaven scale). The duration of marriage and the sexual fulfillment of marriage, in other words, intensify the influence of husband and wife on each other's "stories of God" (just as we have seen in a previous chapter).

TABLE 11.15

**Correlations Between Spouses
by Sexual Fulfillment in Marriage**

(Coefficient of Correlation = Pearson's r)

	God as Mother/Lover	God/Heaven
Both spouses say fulfillment is "excellent"	.45	.32
At least one says other than "excellent"	.22	.08*

* Relationship not significant.

In marriages where the spouse is high on the God/heaven scale, after nine or ten years of marriage a respondent is as likely to be high on the scale as a teenager who has grown up in a family with a devout mother (Table 11.16). Similarly, if the spouse is high on the scale and both husband and wife consider the sexual fulfillment in marriage to be excellent, then the respondent is likely to be as high on the God/heaven scale as a teenager from a family in which there was a devout mother. Ten years of marriage or a sexually-fulfilling marriage with a spouse who is high on the scale, has about the same impact as does contact with a sympathetic priest on a young adult and as a devout mother has on the religious imagination of a teenager.

TABLE 11.16

Religious Imagery by Spouse's Religious Imagery by Duration of Marriage

(Percent high on God/Heaven Scale)

	Spouse high on scale	Spouse low on scale
1–2 years	40	25
3–8 years	27	15
9–10 years	50	18

TABLE 11.17

Religious Imagery by Spouse's Religious Imagery by Sexual Fulfillment

(Percent)

	Spouse high on scale	Spouse low on scale
Both "excellent"	47	14
Other	27	18*

* Difference not significant.

TABLE 11.18

God/Heaven Scale by Perception of Spouse's Influence by Sexual Fulfillment in Marriage

(Percent high on God/Heaven Scale)

	SPOUSE'S RELIGIOUS INFLUENCE IMPORTANT		SPOUSE'S RELIGIOUS INFLUENCE NOT IMPORTANT	
	Spouse high on God/Heaven Scale	Spouse low on God/Heaven Scale	Spouse high on God/Heaven Scale	Spouse low on God/Heaven Scale
Sexual fulfillment of respondent:				
"Excellent"	50	21	33	31
Not "Excellent"	31	18	21	13

TABLE 11.19

Spouse's Influence on God/Heaven Scale by Sex
(Percent high on God/Heaven Scale)

	Spouse high on God/Heaven Scale	Spouse not high on God/Heaven Scale
Spouse is husband	35	14
Spouse is wife	31	20

TABLE 11.20

God/Heaven Scale by Spouse's Religious Image by Sexual Fulfillment in Marriage by Sex
(Percent high on God/Heaven Scale)

	SPOUSE IS HUSBAND		SPOUSE IS WIFE	
	Spouse high on scale	Spouse low on scale	Spouse high on scale	Spouse low on scale
Respondent says sexual fulfillment is "Excellent"	46	12	31	26
Respondent says sexual fulfillment is not "Excellent"	25	17	28	18

TABLE 11.21

God/Heaven Scale for Spouses by Respondent's Religious Images by Sexual Fulfillment in Marriage by Sex
(Percent)

	RESPONDENT IS HUSBAND		RESPONDENT IS WIFE	
	Respondent high on scale	Respondent low on scale	Respondent high on scale	Respondent low on scale
Spouse says sexual fulfillment is "Excellent"	48	25	33	9
Spouse says sexual fulfillment is not "Excellent"	23	21	28	21

The mother and the priest, however, are in all likelihood more or less self-consciously transmitting the post-conciliar religious consciousness. It is less probable that spouses are aware that their "story of God" is something new or something renewed in the Church—though it is not absolutely impossible that there is some self-consciousness operating in the convergence of religious imagery in the marital relationship.

TABLE 11.22

Wives' Score on God/Heaven Scale by Husbands' Score by Duration of Marriage

(Percent high on scale)

Duration	Husbands high on scale	Husbands low on scale
1–5 years	25	21
6–10	35	10

Out-Of-Wedlock Relationships

Highlights

1 *A number of different influences seem to go into the decision about entering out-of-wedlock unions and the factors relate to one another in a fairly complex fashion suggesting that there is no simple explanation of such a choice.*

2 *Persons in out-of-wedlock unions are much more likely to be younger (under twenty-six) than those who are married, to come from families where the family relationships are strained, to come from religiously mixed marriages, and to report an unhappy childhood.*

3 *Those who had more than eight years of Catholic education are three times as likely to be in married unions than in unmarried unions, and are more willing to say that children were important in their life. Those in out-of-wedlock relationships are more likely to say living together before marriage is not wrong, but substantially less likely to be high on a scale of religious imagination which measured their images of God as mother and lover.*

4 *Those living together without being married, while they do not attend weekly liturgies, do not seem to have given up on either God or the Church (Table 12.4).*

5 *Despite their temporary alienation from the Church, persons in out-of-wedlock relationships still tend to see Catholicism as playing an important role in their future (Table 12.5).*

6 *Those persons in out-of-wedlock relationships and those who are married tend to be similar in terms of their participation in some Catholic activities. They still rate Catholicism as highly as those who are married in its value/identity/worship function and are as likely to consider themselves close to their parish as the married.*

Chapter 12

Out-Of-Wedlock Relationships

Approximately 11 percent of the young people in our sample who were not "single" were living in "out-of-wedlock" relationships (together with the 9 percent divorced, this meant that 20 percent of the young Catholics in the sample were not "single," displaying a situation which might well trouble the Church). Approximately the same proportion of out-of-wedlock relationships were reported in English and French Canada.

It is altogether possible that there is underreporting of this population group since those living in such liaisons might not be disposed to fill out a questionnaire (although in five out of fifty-one cases, the "companion" filled out a "spouse's" questionnaire). Thus, analysis presented in this chapter applies to a segment of those in out-of-wedlock relationships, but one cannot say how many of those in such relationships who did not fill out our questionnaire might react differently (though the 80 percent response rate of our study makes it unlikely that we have missed an enormous number of young Catholics in out-of-wedlock arrangements).

It is possible to speculate before the analysis that a number of different factors might go into the decision to enter such a relationship. First of all, the person involved might not believe that the relationship is wrong. Second, the person might be young and perhaps be experimenting before settling down and marrying. Third, the person might be less interested in traditional family values than those Catholics who have contracted to marriage. Fourth, there might have been strain or tension in the family of origin which would make the young person somewhat more hesitant about entering a permanent or quasi-permanent commitment to marry. Finally, that Catholic education and a religious imagination might play a role in explaining the propensity of some young people who enter into such unions.

Table 12.1 (page 159) presents evidence that all or nearly all of the expectations were sustained. A number of different influences seem to go into making the decision about entering out-of-wedlock unions and the factors relate to one another in a fairly complex fashion suggesting that there is no simple explanation of such a choice.

FIGURE 12.1

"Causes" of Out of Wedlock Relationships

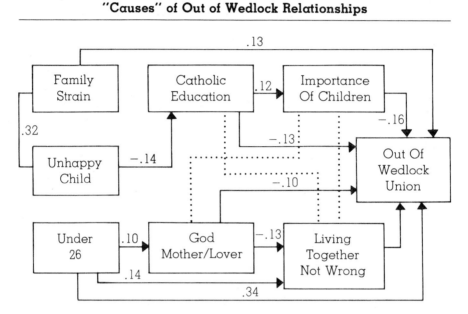

Coefficients on paths which cross from one "causal" system to the other:

Family strain and living together = .14

God as mother and importance of children = .12

Living together and importance of children = −.20

R^2 for living together = .15

R^2 for out of wedlock unions = .32

Those in such unions are much more likely to be younger (under twenty-six) than those who are married, to come from families where the relationships between the parents and between the child and the parents are strained, to come from religiously mixed marriages, and to report an unhappy childhood. Those who had more than eight years of Catholic education were three times as likely to be in married unions as in unmarried unions and there was a 20 percentage point difference between the two in their willingness to say that children were very important "in their life." Those who are in out-of-wedlock unions were also 30 percentage points more likely (80 percent versus 50 percent) to say living together before marriage was never wrong but they were also substantially less likely (31 percent versus 43 percent) to be high on a scale of religious imagination which measured their images of

God as a mother and lover. The "new" religious sensibility represented by this scale does not seem to lead to greater sexual permissiveness but rather to less sexual permissiveness, perhaps because if God is perceived as a mother and lover one is more careful about the love relationships one enters.

TABLE 12.1

Background Variables and Out of Wedlock Relationships
(Percent)

	Wedlock	Out of Wedlock
Under 26	56	82
Family relationships strained[a]	30	44
Parental marriage religiously mixed	26	35
Unhappy childhood	15	26
More than eight years of Catholic school	19	6
Children very important	54	34
God a mother/lover	43	31
Living together before marriage never wrong	50	80

[a] Factor made up of mother-father relation, self-father, self-mother.

Those in out-of-wedlock relationships are almost twice as likely to be under twenty-six and to be either from a family in which the relations were strained or from a family where there was a religious mixed marriage or to have had an unhappy youth (65 percent versus 38 percent). Youthfulness and factors in the family of origin make a major contribution to choice of an out-of-wedlock relationship.

With so many variables apparently related to behavior, it becomes appropriate to use multiple regression analysis to see which variables are important and how they interrelate with one another. However, since only 11 percent of the sample of the "non-single" are in fact in such relationships, multiple regression analysis is impossible because correlation coefficients tend to degenerate when one is working with a proportion as small as 11 percent. Therefore, it was necessary to create a simulated sample with the same number of respondents in wedlock relationships and in out-of-wedlock relationships. In such a simulation it is possible to explain about one-third of the variance between the two groups.

In Table 12.2 (page 161), we have arranged the variables in a rough causal order with age first, then family background, Catholic education or religious imagination, and finally attitude towards family life (importance of children) and the moral judgment about whether living together is wrong. One can then go down the second column of the table and see how much explanation is added by placing in the model each of the new "causal" layers. A quarter of the explained variance (8 percent out of 32 percent) is accounted for by the fact that those in out-of-wedlock relationships are simply younger—suggesting that the lifestyle implied may not be permanent. Another 6 percent of the variance can be accounted for by family background, strained relationships among the mother/father/self triad, and an unhappy childhood. Catholic education contributes another 3 percent to the explanation of the variance and the imagination of God as a mother/lover another 1 percent. Thus age, family background, education, and religious imagination account for about 18 percent of the difference between those in wedlock relationships and those in out-of-wedlock relationships. The remaining 14 percent of the variance explanation concerns the attitude of the respondent toward the importance of children as a life goal and whether the respondent thinks that living together is wrong, the former raising the explained variance 3 percent and the latter 11 percent. One can account for about 21 percent of the variance between the two groups without considering attitudes towards whether living together is wrong. When that attitude is added to the model, explanatory power is raised almost by half.

When the variables are arranged in a flow chart, such as Figure 12.1 (page 158), it becomes possible to see two "causal" systems which seem to contribute to the choice of an out-of-wedlock relationship: a "family" system at the top of the model and a "youth" system at the bottom of the model. Although three paths cross from the top to the bottom, two dynamisms are at least semi-independent of one another. At the top of the model, family strain, an unhappy childhood, a lack of Catholic education, and a lower estimation of the importance of children as a life goal contribute to the decision to enter an out-of-wedlock union. In the bottom half of the model, youthfulness and the conviction that living together is not sinful are the principal factors at work. The God as mother and lover religious "story" plays an interesting role. Young people are more likely to accept that story. The story itself, however, correlates negatively both with approval of living together and with choosing an out-of-wedlock union. But young people are also more likely to choose such unions. Thus, the proportion entering into these liaisons would be even higher if it were not for the propensity among younger people to think of God as a mother and lover. This religious imagination variable, in other words, seems to depress somewhat the relationship between age and out-of-wedlock unions. The correlation with being under twenty-six is .28. However, when the influence of the religious imagination is removed in Figure 12.1 the correlation goes to .34.

Thus their religious imagination acts as a "depressing" variable, masking as it were an even more powerful relationship. More young people, therefore, would be in out-of-wedlock unions if it were not for their religious sensibility to see God as a mother and lover.

TABLE 12.2

Religious Behavior and Attitudes for Out of Wedlock Relationships
(Percent)

	In Wedlock	Out of Wedlock
Mass weekly	33	9
Communion weekly	19	5
Frequent prayer	50	38
Very close to God	43	26
Close to Church	49	28
Close to parish	30	27

In dealing, then, with the dramatically increasing phenomenon of out-of-wedlock unions, the Church is faced for the most part with forces over which it can have little influence. It cannot protect young people from the difficult years between twenty and twenty-six—years of loneliness, confusion, and uncertainty. Nor can it undo the effects of a strained and unhappy childhood. It could indeed build more Catholic schools to affect this lifestyle choice in the future but it cannot provide for Catholic education which was not available in the past. Nor is it likely to be successful in persuading young people that children are more important than they think they are or that living together is not wrong. Perhaps the only way the Church can deal with this lifestyle among young people in their early twenties is to stress even more vigorously than it has the "story" of God as a mother and lover.

The religious practice of those in out-of-wedlock relationships is such as to be appalling to Church leadership. Less than 10 percent of them go to Mass every week, though 5 percent receive communion every week—rather against regulations of the Church, it must be said. However, almost 40 percent pray at least several times a week. Twenty-five percent view themselves as very close to God, 28 percent say that they are either very close or somewhat close to the Church, and an amazing 27 percent say they are either very close or somewhat close to their parish (and in this matter, very similar to those who are in wedlock relationships). Those who are living together without the benefit of marriage are certainly alienated from Church devotional practices but are less likely to feel alienated from God, or from the Church, or from the parish. They may not feel as close to God or as close to the Church as those who are married, but they do not seem to have given up on the Church either. This suggests that they may not be totally unreclaimable by the Church by any means.

They also see considerable value in Catholicism (Table 12.3). Indeed they are more likely than those who are married to say that Catholicism gives them a sense of identity and they show little difference from the married in seeing in Catholicism values to communicate to children, a way of understanding life, and a way of worshiping God. It is almost as if despite their temporary alienation from devotion because of their violation of what they think to be "Church rule" they still see or tend to see Catholicism playing an important role in their future.

TABLE 12.3

Values in Catholicism for Out of Wedlock Relationships
(Percent extremely important)

	In Wedlock	Out of Wedlock
Gives me a sense of identity	7 (40*)	15 (55*)
Gives values to communicate to children	51	42
A way of understanding life	34	31
A way of worshiping God	36	31

* Extremely or somewhat important.

They are also remarkably similar to those in wedlock relationships in their Catholic activities (Table 12.4, page 163). Although they are less likely to have read a Catholic periodical or a Catholic book recently, there are only relatively small differences between those out-of-wedlock and those in wedlock in having talked to priests, made a retreat or day of recollection, watched a Catholic television program, and they are more likely to have participated in a religious discussion group. One-third of them have participated in at least one of such activities (as opposed to 43 percent of those in wedlock) and 16 percent of them have participated in three or more of these activities as against 13 percent of those who are in wedlock. Once again, those the Church would consider "living in sin" do not seem to be all that alienated from the Church. Indeed, many of them seem almost to be leaning over backwards to leave open the paths by which they might return.

Youthfulness, problems in the family of origin, conviction that premarital experimentation is not wrong, the tendency to minimize the importance of children, lack of Catholic education, and a religious imagination that does not stress the role of God as a mother and lover—these seem to be important factors contributing to the decision of many young Catholics to enter nonmarital liaisons. Their devotional practice suffers as a result of these liaisons as does to some extent their sense of being close to God and the Church. Yet they still rate Catholicism as highly as those who are married in its value/identity/worship function and are as likely to engage in a number of Catholic "linking" activities. They are surely not a group of young people the Church can take for granted; but neither are they a group about which the Church ought to despair.

TABLE 12.4

Catholic Activities and Out of Wedlock Relationships
(Percent)

	In Wedlock	Out of Wedlock
Talked to priest	13	14
Made a retreat	5	4
Day of Recollection	4	6
Catholic periodical	29	12
Catholic book	18	12
Catholic TV program	14	14
Home liturgy	5	2
Discussion group	8	12
At least one of the above	43	33
Three or more of the above	13	16

Feminism and the Young Catholic

Highlights

1 *Feminism in this context is understood as the propensity to blur the distinction between the male and female role. It is operationalized by three variables: the conviction that women should be ordained; the belief that a working mother does not harm the child; the propensity to see "having children" as a less important life goal.*

2 *While women are substantially more likely than men to say that having children is extremely important, half of this sample of young women did not see it as "extremely important" and one quarter rated it as "not too important" or "not important at all" (Table 13.1).*

3 *"Feminist" attitudes among young women have a considerable negative effect on religious behavior (Table 13.2).*

4 *The principal correlate of "feminism" is education: the woman's education, her mother's, and her father's (Table 13.3).*

5 *Young Catholic women "feminists" are well-educated, politically liberal, and have had good relationships with their mothers. Their "feminist" attitudes have a negative effect on religious devotion only if there is a low level of confidence in Church leaders (Table 13.4).*

6 *The "feminist" is as likely to be in a satisfying marriage as the non-feminist. While she attaches less importance to children than do other women, the "feminist" Catholic expects to have a larger family than do other young Americans.*

7 *"Feminism" affects confidence, identification, and devotion—it does not affect religious imagination.*

Chapter 13

Feminism and the Young Catholic

The purpose of this chapter is to explore the origins and implications of "feminism" among young Catholic women. The "feminism" can mean many things; in this chapter its meaning is very specific and no other meaning ought to be read into the analysis. "Feminism" is here understood as the *propensity to blur the distinction between the male and the female role.* (It may very well mean many other things in the world beyond this definition, but if one is to attempt any analysis at all, one must specifically define what one means in the analysis.) Furthermore, the blurring of roles is operationalized in this chapter by three variables: 1) the conviction that it is important that women should be ordained, 2) the belief that a working mother does not harm the child, and 3) the propensity to see "having children" as a less important life goal. Women are expected traditionally to think that having children is very important. To the extent that they are likely to attribute less importance to it and to seek importance in their life elsewhere, they are blurring the distinctions between men and women.

In Table 13.1 (page 168) we note that women are still substantially more likely (16 percentage points) than men to say that having children is extremely important. However, half of the young women in our sample did not see having children as extremely important and one-quarter rated it as either "not too important" or "not important at all." It is particularly at the bottom of the scale that the differences between men and women on the importance of children do seem to blur. Twenty-nine percent of the young men and 20 percent of the young women in the sample think that having children is not too important at all.

Women are more likely than men, however, to think that women should be ordained and also more likely than men to think that a working mother does not harm a child (more than half of our women respondents grew up in families where the mother worked during the grammar school and/or high school years). Thus, when the three items are combined into a factor there is virtually no difference in scores of men and women.

TABLE 13.1

"Feminism" Indicators by Sex
(Percent)

	Men	Women
Having children is very important	32	48
Women should be ordained	42	47
A working mother does not harm a child	59	66

"Feminist" attitudes among young women have a considerable negative effect on religious behavior. Those who are at the upper half of the "feminisms" are less likely to attend Mass every week (30 percent as opposed to 50 percent), to receive communion (20 percent as opposed to 33 percent), and pray at least several times a week (34 percent as against 46 percent). They are also much more vigorous supporters of abortion, being almost twice as likely to approve of abortion simply on the grounds that the woman wants no more children. They are 10 percentage points less likely to be close to God and half as likely as those low on the "feminisms" to say they are close to the Church and close to their parish. On the other hand, they are only somewhat different (6 percent) from other women in thinking that parish priests are sympathetic, and 75 percent of them approve of the way their pastor is handling his job. Half of them, as opposed to 20 percent of those who are low in the scale, also think of themselves as politically liberal (Table 13.2, page 169).

How do women make a choice for these values which seem to have such a negative effect on their religious devotion and allegiance? We could find no relation between the family structure in the family of origin and "feminist" attitudes. Those who are high on our scale do not come from unhappy, strained, or tension-filled families. On the contrary, the principal correlate of "feminism" is education: the woman's education, her mother's, and her father's. In addition, a woman who has a managerial or a professional skill and whose mother has worked during her teens (Table 13.3, page 169) is more likely to be "feminist." Finally, a woman who grew up in a family where her relationship with the mother was marked by closeness, strong maternal religious influence, with a mother who was religiously devout and involved in family decisions, is also more likely to be "feminist." Strong education, strong mother, and strong liberal political leanings seem to be the factors that turn a young woman into a "feminist" and explain about a fifth of the variance of the "feminism" role.

TABLE 13.2

Religious Attitudes and Behaviors of Women by "Feminism" Scale
(Women Only)
(Percent)

	Low on the scale	High on the scale
Weekly Mass	50	30
Weekly Communion	33	20
Frequent prayer	46	34
Approve abortion/defective child	80	88
Approve abortion/no more children wanted	26	59
Close to God	50	40
Close to Church	24	13
Close to parish	20	10
Alienated from Church	48	67
Parish priests sympathetic	36	30
Sermons excellent	19	13
Approve pastor's job	80	73

All differences are statistically significant.

TABLE 13.3

Correlations With "Feminism" Scale
(Women Only)
(Coefficient of Correlation = Pearson's r)

Woman's occupation	.19
Woman's education	.31
Father's education	.22
Mother's education	.18
Mother worked during respondent's teens	.10
"Maternity" scale [a]	.12
"Liberal" politically	.26
R = .43	
R² = .19	

[a] Close to mother, mother involved in family decisions, mother strong religious influence, mother frequent Communion.

In Figure 13.1 (page 170), we see that the father's education and the woman's own education as well as her political views are the principal predictors for being a "feminist." Her mother's education affects her through her own education but not directly. However, a relationship with her mother, as measured by the maternity scale, does have a direct influence on her "feminist" attitudes. Today's young Catholic women "feminists" are well-educated and come from well-educated families. They are politically liberal and have had good relationships with their mothers. Their family background is not troubled or irreligious, yet they themselves, as we have seen, tend to be less devout. Granted their low levels of devotion, however, they give their parish priests rather high approval ratings.

FIGURE 13.1

"Causes" of Feminism

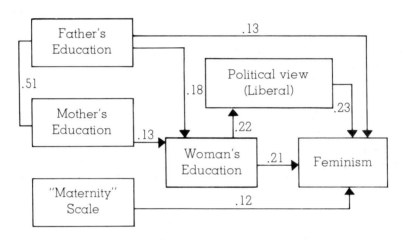

R² = .19

"Feminist" attitudes do not seem to have a depressant effect on religious devotion, however (Table 13.4, page 171), unless a young woman displays low levels of confidence in Church leaders. Thus, if the young woman is confident in Church leadership, her attitudes on the blurring of male and female roles have little effect on her Church attendance. It is only among those who have "some" or "not very much" confidence that one gets a statistically significant difference between those who are in the bottom half and those who are in the top half of the "feminism" scale, with a latter group only half as likely as the former to attend church weekly. It is, in other words, precisely the combination of low confidence in religious leadership and "feminist" attitudes which leads to devotional alienation.

This phenomenon is also illustrated in Table 13.5 (page 171). Negative correlations between "feminism" and Church attendance and "feminism" and closeness to the Church are cut in half when one takes into account the problems that many "feminist" young women have with Church authority. If Church leadership could reestablish confidence among these young women, the alienation might not be so severe—though given the attitudes toward sex and particularly towards abortion of the "feminist" young women, a reestablishment of the confidence might be difficult.

TABLE 13.4

"Feminist" Attitudes, Feelings About Church Authorities and Church Attendances
(Women Only)
(Percent regular Mass attenders)

	Low on "Feminism"	High on "Feminism"
Confident in church leaders	67	66
Not confident in church leaders	43*	22

* Significantly different from those who are high on "feminism."

TABLE 13.5

Correlations Between "Feminism" and Church Attendance and Closeness to Church
(Women Only)
(Coefficient of Correlation = Pearson's r)

	Simple Correlation	Correlation With Church Authority Problems Taken into Account
Feminism and regular church	−.20	−.10
Feminism and closeness to church	−.25	−.12

Just as their "feminism" cannot be explained by problems in the family of origin, so too "feminism" does not seem to create any particular problems in the family of procreation (Table 13.6 and 13.7, page 172). According both to her report and her husband's report, the "feminist" young Catholic is as likely to be in a satisfying marriage as her opposite number on the lower half of the "feminism" scale.

Finally, while she attaches less importance to children than do other women, the "feminist" young Catholic expects to have a larger family than do other young Americans (2.4 children) even though her expectations are somewhat smaller than those young Catholic women less likely to have a "feminist" orientation (Table 13.8, page 172). They do not seem to be any less successful as wives or any less likely to be mothers. Yet, they are committed to a blurring of the role distinction between men and women and this commitment, caused mostly by education and a liberal political viewpoint, puts them at odds with Church leadership and leads to much lower levels of religious devotion.

TABLE 13.6

"Feminism" and Marital Satisfaction
(Percent very satisfied)

	Low on Feminism Scale	High on Feminism Scale
Woman's report	64	61
Her husband's report	69	70

TABLE 13.7

"Feminism" and Sexual Fulfillment in Marriage
(Percent "Excellent")

	Low on Feminism Scale	High on Feminism Scale
Woman's report	47	47
Husband's report	38	39

TABLE 13.8

Number of Children Expected for Married Respondents

Low on Feminism Scale	2.8
High on Feminism Scale	2.4*

* Difference statistically significant.

What proportion of Catholic young women can be said to have their religious behavior notably influenced by "feminist" attitudes? Table 13.9 (page 173) shows that about one-third of them score quite high on the scale and are very notably affected while another 36 percent are somewhat influenced by the "feminists," and a remaining 30 percent who are quite low on the "feminist" scale did not seem to be influenced by "feminist" attitudes. Only a quarter of the first group go to church weekly. Two-fifths of the second group and half of the third group go to church weekly. Forty-five percent of the low "feminist" women consider themselves alienated from the Church as do 50 percent of the moderate "feminists," and 67 percent of those who are quite high on the "feminism" scale. Two-thirds of Catholic young women experience some negative impact on their religious behavior of "feminist" attitudes and another one-fifth have experienced substantial impact on their religious devotion and affiliation because of the "feminist" positions.

TABLE 13.9

What Proportion of Young Catholic Women are "Feminists"?				
(Percent)				
	Church attendance (almost weekly)	N	Alienated from the Church (slightly close or not close at all)	Proportion
−2 and −1 on "Feminism" scale	51	(143)	45	33
0 on the scale	44	(173)	52	36
+1 and +2 on the scale	27	(164)	67	34
				100

Many of these young women may not consider themselves explicitly to be "feminists." The point in the present analysis is not what label is pinned on them or they pin on themselves (hence the word is always used in quotes), but that there is an orientation that one may call "feminist" which emphasizes the blurring of the distinction between male and female role and this orientation has very substantial religious impact on a considerable number of young Catholic women.

It is possible to replicate many of the findings reported in this chapter by looking at the entire adult population of Catholic women as represented by NORC's *General Social Survey* (GSS). The four "feminist" measures are entirely different—women should take care of the home and let the running of the country to men; a woman should not work when her husband can support her; the respondent would not vote for a woman as President; and women are not suited for politics. We note in Table 13.10 (page 174) that only on the second item is there a significant difference between women and men.

The same pattern of the effect of low confidence in religious leadership can be observed in Table 13.11 (page 174) that we discussed in Table 13.4. It is precisely those women who have low confidence in Church leadership and are high on the "feminist" scale that are least likely to go to church. Those "feminists" who have high confidence in Church leadership are not different in their church attendance from the "non-feminists." The proportions are higher in Table 13.11 because older women are more likely to go to church than are younger women. However, the pattern is the same as in Table 13.4.

TABLE 13.10

"Feminist" Measures from General Social Survey by Sex
(Percent)

	Men	Women
Women should take care of the home; let men take care of country	32	32
Women should not work if husbands can support them	36	28
Would vote for woman president	83	82
Women are not suited for politics	43	45*

* Difference statistically significant.

TABLE 13.11

Church Attendance by Confidence in Church Leadership and "Feminist" Attitudes (GENSOC)
(Women Only)
(Percent almost weekly Church attendance)

	Low on "Feminism"	High on "Feminism"
High on confidence	76	71
Low on confidence	59	44

A basically similar causal pattern can be found in the GSS sample as was reported in the young adult sample. In Figure 13.1 and in Table 13.3, the "feminists" and the entire Catholic women population are especially likely to be educated and to come from well-educated families (Table 13.12 and Figure 13.2, page 175). While there are somewhat different patterns in Figure 13.2 than in Figure 13.1 (mother's education influence is more important in Figure 13.2 and the father's more important in Figure 13.1), both models explain the same amount of the variance—about one-fifth—in the "feminist" attitudes of Catholic women.

If one looks at Catholic women in research from the GSS, the same population has different responses from those studied in the Catholic young adult project (Table 13.13, page 175). One finds almost exactly the same relationship between "feminism" and church attendance—about 20 percentage points difference between the two groups in almost weekly church attendance (that in the GSS, women in their twenties are 5 percentage points higher is probably the result of a slightly different wording in the question).

TABLE 13.12

Correlations Between "Feminism" and Background Variables (GENSOC)

(Women Only)
(Coefficient of Correlation = Pearson's r)

Education	.41
Mother's education	.31
Father's education	.28
Political liberalism	.08

FIGURE 13.2

Education "Causes" of Feminism

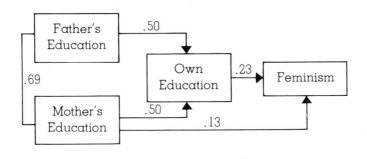

$R^2 = .19$

TABLE 13.13

Church Attendance and Church Alienation for Feminists under 30 (GENSOC)

(Women Only)
(Percent)

	Low on "Feminism"	High on "Feminism"
Church weekly	56	35
Alienated (a not very strong Catholic)	52	65

But it is not merely women under thirty who experience a negative impact of "feminism" on their religious devotion. As Table 13.14 (page 176) shows, the negative relationship persists, though not as dramatically, for Catholic women under fifty. It is only for women born before 1930 that "feminism" does not seem to depress levels of religious devotion.

TABLE 13.14

Church Attendance and Church Alienation for "Feminists" by Age (GENSOC)
(Women Only)
(Percent)

	Low on "Feminism"	High on "Feminism"
Under 50:		
Church weekly	58	48
Alienated (not a very "strong" Catholic)	49	57
Over 50:		
Church weekly	76	78
Alienated (not a very "strong" Catholic)	32	30

Finally, Table 13.15 shows that according to the GSS, 60 percent of the Catholic women under thirty fall into the category in which it can be said the "feminism" influences negatively their religious behavior (as opposed to 65 percent in the young adult study—virtually the same proportion despite entirely different "feminist" measures). Slightly over half of the Catholic women under fifty fall into the same category, for only a fifth of the Catholic women over fifty can be rated as "feminists" and in that group there is no impact of "feminist" attitudes on religious devotion.

TABLE 13.15

Feminists by Age
(Women Only)
(Percent)

Age	Proportion
Under 50	52
Over 50	21
Under 30	60

One is forced to conclude from this chapter the melancholy fact that learning of gender roles is a very considerable problem for the

Church and its ministry, not only to women in their twenties but to all Catholic women born since 1930. And for the young and the not-so-young, a lack of confidence in Church leaders seems to be a substantial part of the problem. It is worth noting, incidentally, that the ordination of women is not one of the indicators in the GSS data. One might, therefore, legitimately argue that while the ordination of women is an important symbolic issue, it is not necessary to fall back on it to explain the problem the Church is experiencing with the female half of its population under fifty. Rather, it is the blurring of the gender roles (for which the ordination of women is an excellent symbolic indicator) that a substantial proportion of women see as the real issue—and the lack of understanding of this issue by Church leadership as the real problem.

It will also be noted in Table 13.13 that the alienation from the Church of "feminists" measured in that table by the proportion who in the GSS describe themselves as "not very strong Catholics" and the alienation in Table 13.2 measured by those who say they are not very close to the Church is virtually the same for respondents under thirty. Of those who are low on "feminism" in the GSS, 52 percent say they are not very strong Catholics while of those who are very high on "feminism," 65 percent make that assertion. The percentages on a differently-worded question measuring the same general dimension of alienation from the Church are seen in Table 13.2.

Is the alienation of Catholic women both in the under thirty and under fifty generations a phenomenon to be found in all religious denominations or is it uniquely Catholic? Analysis of the data in the NORC GSS (Tables 13.16—13.18, page 178) suggests that the phenomenon is neither universal nor uniquely Catholic. "Feminism" leads to a higher score on religious alienation (the proportion saying they are not "strong" in the denomination for Baptists and to some extent for Lutherans, but not for Methodists). Similarly, "feminism" makes a considerable difference in the proportion of Baptists and Catholics who have little confidence in their religious leadership, but relatively little difference for Methodists and Lutherans. (Our analysis is limited to these three denominations because only these three have sufficient numbers of respondents to permit investigation in the GSS data.) Futhermore (Table 13.19, page 179), among the Baptists, but not among the Methodists, it is precisely among those that are high on "feminism" and lack great confidence in religious leaders that the lowest levels of church attendance are to be found, a pattern exactly similar to that observed among Catholics. Baptists and Catholic women, but not Methodists (and presumably not Lutherans), who are high on measures of "feminism" are less likely to go to church precisely because they are more likely to have little confidence in Church leadership. It is reasonable to conclude, therefore, that they see their Church leadership as an obstacle to their "feminist" aspirations. The problem that exists in some denominations but not in others implies the women membership of some denominations, Catholic and Baptist for example, perceive their leaders as opposed to equality for women and committed to the maintenance of the old gender roles. In other denominations where leaders are not so perceived, women are not alienated from the denomination.

TABLE 13.16

Weekly or Almost Weekly Church
by "Feminism" for Major Denominations
(Percent)

	Low on "Feminism"	High on "Feminism"
Baptists	59	43
	N = (412)	N = (174)
Methodists	51	49
	N = (216)	N= (111)
Lutherans	50	48
	N = (150)	N = (86)

TABLE 13.17

Church Alienation for "Feminists" by Major Denomination
(Percent not "strong")

	Low on "Feminism"	High on "Feminism"
Baptists	47	60
Methodists	59	63
Lutherans	40	46

TABLE 13.18

Confidence in Religious Leaders by "Feminism"
for Major Denominations
(Percent a great deal)

	Low on "Feminism"	High on "Feminism"
Baptists	45	27
Methodists	43	40
Lutherans	45	41
(Catholics)	42	30

TABLE 13.19

Attendance at Church by "Feminism" by Confidence in Religious Leadership for Baptists and Methodists

(Percent)

	Confidence Not "Great"		Confidence "Great"	
	Low on "Feminism"	High on "Feminism"	Low on "Feminism"	High on "Feminism"
Baptists	55	39	63	57
	N = (217)	(118)	(176)	(46)
Methodists	46	39	59	61
	N = (115)	(66)	(88)	(43)

It must be repeated that the measures of "feminism" used both from the *Young Catholics* Survey and the GSS are moderate. They do not represent radical ideological positions. They represent "feminism" and not FEMINISM. Most of the "feminist" women are married, as happily married as "non-feminists," and many are mothers. Many of them probably would not even think of themselves as "feminists," but they do object to the traditional rigid distinctions in gender roles, and in the case of Catholics, see their Church leadership committed to preserving such distinctions.

However, the fact that the Baptists also have the problem suggests that such questions as birth control, divorce, the ordination of women, and the celibate leadership of the Catholic Church may be peripheral to the disdain for Church leadership found among many younger and better-educated Catholic women—the Baptists have a married clergy, permit women ministering, and do not have strong stands against divorce or birth control. The alienation of Catholic women from their Church on gender roles, then, does not seem to be a matter of specific issues peculiar to Catholicism, but rather reflects generalized perceptions of Church leadership's determination to keep women in second-class positions.

This concept does not impinge in the religious imagination, however—there is no significant correlate between the religious imagination of members and "feminist" attitudes. Those with benign stories of grace, in other words, are as likely to be "feminists" as they are to be traditionalists. "Feminism" affects confidence, identification, and devotion. It does not affect religious imagination. It is, nonetheless, a very serious problem for Catholic Church leaders because their perceived commitment to continuing traditional gender roles has "turned off" half of the mothers who are today rearing children.

In a way, this chapter is the most melancholy in our entire report. One must say candidly that Church leadership has not faced the fact that "feminism" is not merely Sister Kane confronting the Pope, nor the small number of nuns who wish to be ordained. It is not merely the anti-family lesbians who wish to take control of the White House Conference of Families. Two-thirds of the Catholic women under thirty and half of those under fifty are notably influenced by attitudes which could properly be called "feminist" (though the women may often not choose to use the term).

These attitudes have a negative impact on their religious behavior especially because such attitudes cause them to have very little confidence in Church leadership. Most of the women, indeed virtually all, could not be called "radical feminists." They are married women with children whose family relationships are at least as satisfying as those who are not "feminists." Church leadership may be able to dismiss the radicals. It would, however, dismiss "feminists" in the Church at very considerable peril to the future of American Catholicism.

The Confidant Relationship

Highlights

1   *Catholic married women often have helpful relationships with their local clergy, the sort that cannot be found in other religious denominations.*

2   *The celibate priest is a positive asset to the marriage relationship (Table 14.2). If a woman's relationship with a priest is both recent and influential, the joint marital satisfaction is high (Table 14.4).*

3   *Without the intervention of a priest, confidence in Church leadership correlates negatively with marital satisfaction (Table 14.8). This is not statistically significant for other denominations. The celibacy of the priest is not an obstacle to explaining the "confidant" relationship and it may be a positive advantage.*

4   *A wife's marital satisfaction is improved by a confidant relationship with a priest precisely because that relationship tends to enhance the sexual fulfillment of her husband.*

5   *"Confidant" relationships exist in parishes which are active and have democratic leadership, where the counseling skills are excellent, and where the priests are pious, committed, and well-trained.*

6   *The confidant relationship has an effect on a young Catholic married woman's attitudes towards change in the clerical life. Such women are more "liberal," seeing change as important. They support the ordination of women priests but favor the retention of clerical celibacy. The exact pattern exists among their husbands (Table 14.15).*

Chapter 14

The Confidant Relationship

While Catholic women with "feminist" propensity are alienated from Church leadership, they do not seem to be alienated from their own local clergy. It would appear from the argument presented in this chapter that the antagonism is towards the "hierarchy," perhaps even towards the "Vatican," but not toward the lower clergy. On the contrary, it seems that Catholic married women have helpful relationships with their local clergy, the sort that cannot be found in other religious denominations.

There are virtually no differences between women and men (whether married or unmarried) in their judgments as to whether their parish priest is very sympathetic, and in their having had a conversation with a priest about a religious problem during the past year and saying that a priest has had a considerable impact on their thinking about the Catholic faith (Table 14.1, page 184).

The last two items were combined into a factor, which taps both recent conversations with a priest and agreement that a priest has had a powerful religious effect on one's life. (It cannot be argued that the priests are the same person.) The scale correlates positively (Table 14.2, page 184) with marital satisfaction, both for the wife and for the family unit. If a woman is high on the scale, both she and her husband are more likely to say that their marriage is very satisfactory. Far from being a rival to the husband, then, it would appear that the celibate priest is a positive asset to his marriage relationship.

This effect seems only to exist for women (Table 14.3, page 185). The more likely a woman is to have an influential and recent relationship with a priest, the more likely she is to be very satisfied with her marriage, while a man's relationship with a priest does not increase the quality of his marital satisfaction. However, the woman's relationship does increase the joint satisfaction of husband and wife with their marriage. If the woman has neither had a recent conversation with a priest nor has been strongly influenced religiously in her life by a priest, only half the couples

183

will both say they are very satisfied with their marriage. If her relationship with a priest is both recent and influential, however, 72 percent of the couples will say they are very satisfied with their marriage. Note that (Table 14.4, page 185) both recentness and strong influence are required for the effect on joint marital satisfaction (the "high" score on the scale). One without the other makes little difference in marital satisfaction for husband and wife.

TABLE 14.1

Women's Attitudes Towards Priestly Performance by Marital Status
(Percent)

	Women		Men	
	Married	Unmarried	Married	Unmarried
Percent parish priest very sympathetic	35	31	35	36
Percent talk religious problem with priest last year	15	15	9	12
Percent talks with priest affected thinking about Catholicism "very much"	19	20	16	14

TABLE 14.2

Correlations Between Marital Satisfaction and Woman's Spiritual Relationship with a Priest [a]
(Coefficient of Correlation = Pearson's r)

	Wife "Very Satisfied"	Both spouses "Very Satisfied" with marriage
Priest relationship	.17*	.13*

[a] Scale composed of recent conversation with a priest, and priest exercise a great influence on religious thinking.
* Both relationships are statistically significant.

The "confidant" relationship also correlates with positive psychological well-being (Table 14.5, page 185) significantly for women and not significantly for men, but only (Table 14.6, page 186) for married women, a little more than one-third of whom are high on the positive psychological well-being scale if they have no contact with a priest, and almost two-thirds of whom are high on the scale if they have a confidant relationship.

One out of every seven married Catholic women is high on the relationship with a priest scale, which is to say that she has a priest "confidant"—she has had a recent conversation with the priest about religious matters and reports that a priest has had an important religious influence on her life. Such women are likely to be higher on the score of positive well-being and to be involved in marriages in which both the wife and husband are satisfied with the quality of the relationship.

TABLE 14.3

Marital Satisfaction by Relationship with Priest
(Percent "very satisfied")

	Women	Men
Priest scale	55	74
	(91)	(58)
Low	64	70
	(137)	(90)
High	74	71
	(35)	(17)

TABLE 14.4

Marital Satisfaction of Both Husband and Wife by Wife's Relationship with Priest
(Percent of couples in which both say they are "very satisfied")

Priest scale	50
	(72)
Low	53
	(99)
to	
High	72
	(29)

TABLE 14.5

Correlation Between Psychological Well-Being (Positive Happiness) and Relationship with a Priest by Sex for Married People
(Coefficient of Correlation = Pearson's r)

Men	Women
.06*	.15**

* Not significant.
** Significant.

The question naturally arises as to whether this apparently satisfactory relationship happens despite the celibacy of the priest or because of it. Can such relationships be found in other denominations?

TABLE 14.6

Psychological Well-Being by Relationship with Priest by Sex and Marital Status

(Percent high on the Positive Happiness Scale)

	Women		Men	
	Married	Single	Married	Single
Relationship with priest	37	48	41	39
low	42	52	46	56
to				
high	64*	50	53	55

* This is the only column in the table expressing a statistically significant relationship.

Since the data in the *General Social Survey* provide no methods for directly addressing this question, one must use an indirect and tentative argument which is presented as speculative exploration and not a certain proof.

Young Catholic women who have high confidence in their organizational leadership (Table 14.7, page 187) are more likely to say that they are very satisfied with their marriage than those who have low confidence in their religious leadership. However, this seems to be entirely the result of the fact that some such women have a confidant relationship with a priest (Table 14.8, page 187). One may observe in Table 14.8 in the right-hand column that those who lack a confidant relationship and have a great deal of confidence in Church leadership are lower in marital satisfaction than those who have low confidence in Church leadership. Without the intervention of a priest, confidence in Church leadership correlates negatively with marital satisfaction for Catholic women. If you are very confident in Church leadership, your marriage is less satisfactory unless there is a priest "confidant" involved who seems to be able to reverse the direction of the relationship.

Returning to the GSS, we find (Table 14.9, page 187) that the significant positive correlation between confidence in Church leadership and marital satisfaction for women exists only among Roman Catholics. It is not statistically significant for the other denominations. Now since we have already determined that the reason why there is a positive relationship between marital satisfaction and confidence in Church leadership for Catholic married women is the intervention of a priest confidant, we may speculate that the absence of a significant relationship in the other denominations may well be the result of an absence of an intervening clerical confidant. Minimally it can be said with confidence that the celibacy of the priest is not an obstacle to explaining the confidant relationship and there are strong hints that it may be a positive asset.

TABLE 14.7

Marital Satisfaction for Women by Confidence in Organizational Leadership
(Percent very satisfied)

Confidence high	62
Confidence low	57

TABLE 14.8

Marital Satisfaction by Confidence in Church Leadership by Relationship with a Priest for Catholic Women
(Percent high on marital satisfaction)

	Priest Relationship	
	High	Low
Confidence in leadership:		
High	68	52
Low	57	61

TABLE 14.9

Family Satisfaction for Married Women by Confidence in Church Leadership (General Social Survey)
(Percent Very Satisfied)

	Catholics	Baptists	Methodists	Lutherans
Confidence high	43	41	47	45
Confidence low	33	36	41	41
Gamma	.20	.09	.13	.10
Significance	.008	n.s.	n.s.	n.s.
Percent with high confidence	51 (800)	47 (643)	49 (371)	53 (282)

One might further speculate that for Catholic young married women a friendly and trusting relationship with another man in which there is little "danger" and considerable encouragement, social support, and reassurance, leaves her more free and less tense for the relationship with her husband. It may well be that the ability to provide such relationships for married women is one of the unperceived but important functions of clerical celibacy (it might be added that those of us who have worked as parish priests have intuitively been aware of this function for a long time). It also may be that the absence of a counterpart relationship for young Catholic married men could be a pragmatic argument for the ordination of women—though if our speculative reasons about the importance of celibacy for such relationships is correct, then it would follow that this function would only be achieved with a celibate women clergy.

TABLE 14.10

Correlations Between "Priest Confidant" and "Sexual Fulfillment"
(Coefficient of Correlation = Pearson's r)

Wife	Husband
.04*	.11

* Not significant.

What is there about a confidant relationship between a priest and a young married woman which facilitates the marital happiness of both her and her husband? While the confidant relationship does indeed correlate with "stories of grace," it is not the intervening variable that explains the link between a priest confidant and a fulfilled marriage. Nor (Table 14.10) does a confidant relationship improve the woman's estimate of the sexual fulfillment in her marriage. However, it does improve her husband's propensity to say that the sexual fulfillment is excellent. A confidant relationship correlates not with the wife's sexual fulfillment but with the husband's. If the woman has what may well be a supportive friendship with a priest, it improves the quality of her husband's sexual satisfaction. Furthermore (Table 14.11, page 189), when these three variables are put into a regression equation it develops that the sexual fulfillment of the husband is indeed the intervening variable linking the confidant relationship with a priest and the marital satisfaction of the wife. A wife's marital satisfaction is improved by a confidant relationship with a priest precisely because that relationship tends to enhance the sexual fulfillment of her husband.

A possible explanation for this phenomenon is that the young wife receives sufficient encouragement from the priest to be open to sexuality that she abandons some of her inhibitions and is able, therefore, to be a more satisfying sexual partner to her husband. If such be the dynamics of the relationship—and they certainly ought to be examined much more closely in future research—one has an interesting manifestation of a "latent function" of clerical celibacy and also perhaps another pragmatic argument for the importance of a counterpart "confidant" for married men.

TABLE 14.11

Relationships Among Wife's Marital Satisfaction, Husband's Sexual Fulfillment, and "Priest Confidant"

(Dependent variable = Wife's marital satisfaction)

	Simple Correlation r	Standardized Correlation beta
"Priest Confidant"	.10	.05*
Husband's Sexual Fulfillment	.29	.28

* Not significant.

What kind of priest do such women seek out for confidant relationships? Those in such relationships are much more likely to rate priest's sermons as excellent, to describe priests as very understanding, to be in parishes where there is a good deal of activity, and where priests do not expect laity to be followers. They are also substantially more likely to endorse the piety, concern, and the training of their professional clergy (Table 14.12, page 190). It would appear that the confidant relationships exist in parishes which are active and have democratic leaderships, where the counseling skills are excellent and where the priests are pious, committed, and well-trained. Presumably these are precisely the kind of qualities a young woman would look for in the priest "confidant."

When the ratings of priest performance are subjected to a factor analysis, two scales emerge—one that measured the social and political activism of a priest, and the other his piety, concern, professional preparation, and democratic style. The social activism factor correlated neither positively nor negatively with the confidant relationship (Table 14.13, page 190). However, the "professionalism" of the priest did correlate positively and significantly: the women who are high on the scale estimating the "professionalism" of their parish clergy were twice as likely to have confidant relationships (Table 14.14, page 190).

(There was no relationship between "feminism" and "confidant" relationship. Those who are high on the "feminism" scale and those who were low were equally as likely to have such a relationship. Young women's perception that Church leadership wishes to keep them in an inferior status does not seem to have any effect on their propensity to enter confidant relationships with the priests).

TABLE 14.12

View of Clergy of Married Women by Whether They Have a "Confidant" Relationship or Not

(Percent)

	"Confidant"	
	Yes	No
Sermons excellent	33	10
Priest very understanding	50	32
Active parish	62	50
Priests expect laity to be followers (disagree strongly)	32	13
Seminaries not training priests well (disagree strongly)	52	35
Priests not as pious as they used to be (disagree strongly)	29	13
Priests only concerned about selves (disagree strongly)	58	44

TABLE 14.13

Confidant Relationships by Priest Evaluation Factors

(Coefficient of Correlation = Pearson's r)

Priest as Social Activist	Priestly Professionalism
.02*	.13

* Not significant.

TABLE 14.14

Attitudes Towards Change in the Clergy by Whether a Married Woman has a Priest "Confidant"

(Percent very or somewhat important)

	"Confidant"	
	Yes	No
Ordain women priests	55	40
Permit priests to marry	48	60

The materials presented in this chapter are extremely tentative. We do not know, for example, that the priests with whom the married woman has talked recently is the same priest who has had a notable impact on her life. Nor can we be sure that celibacy is an asset developing the clergyman/woman relationship. Finally, it is possible that it is precisely those women who are in satisfactory marriages and whose husbands are satisfied with the quality of the sexual relationship who would feel free to choose a religious relationship with a priest, so the causal connection may flow in the opposite direction than the one assumed in this chapter. This seems less likely than the relationship postulated in the chapter but certainly cannot be excluded until further research is done. Nevertheless, despite their antagonism towards higher Church leaders, it is clear that young Catholic married women are able to have satisfying relationships with their priests, relationships which are at least linked to, if indeed do not promote, happier marriages.

What effect does a confidant relationship have on a young Catholic married woman's attitudes towards change in the clerical life? Such women are more "liberal" than those who lack such relationships on the matter of ordination of women. Fifty-five percent of them think such a change is important as opposed to 40 percent of those without a confidant. On the other hand, they are less likely (Table 14.14) to support permission for a married clergy—48 percent of the "confidant" women support such a change as opposed to 60 percent of those who lack a confidant.

Clearly the confidant women are not reactionaires on the subject of women priests, yet they favor the retention of clerical celibacy, perhaps because they perceive—however dimly—that their own beneficial relationship with a priest is in part the result of his celibate status. Perhaps one of the reasons why they strongly support the other change is that they perceive that their husbands might benefit from a similar relationship with a celibate woman priest.

Furthermore—and perhaps astonishingly—exactly the same pattern exists among the husbands (Table 14.15, page 192). Those with wives in confidant relationships are more likely to support the ordination of women and less likely than those whose wives lack such relationships to advocate optional celibacy—as though they too perceive the enhancement to their lives of a celibate priest counselor for their wives—and perhaps even the additional enhancement which would occur if they had a celibate woman priest as their own "confidant."

Obviously these speculations are very tentative, but they point in the direction of inquiries which are extremely important for the future of the priesthood and the future of the Church.

The final question to be asked is whether it is precisely those husbands and wives who have benefited from the confidant relationship who are the most likely to be in favor of celibacy and also in favor of the ordination of women. Are those whose marriages have been positively affected by a wife's relationship with a priest most reluctant to see celibacy abandoned but also most eager to have women priests (from whom, possibly, men can derive similar benefits as their wives have from relationships with celibate priests)?

TABLE 14.15

Attitudes of Husbands Towards Change in the Clergy by Whether Their Wives Have a "Confidant" Relationship with a Priest

(Percent)

	Wife has a "Confidant"	Wife does not have a "Confidant"
Support ordination of women	60	43
Support married priests	50	58

Admittedly this is a very long-shot question. It supposes that the relationship demonstrated in the previous tables is to be found only among those whose marriages have profited from confidant relationships and that for others in which there is a confidant relationship the situation will reverse itself. It assumes that if a table is created in which those who are in confidant relationships (or whose wives are) and those who are high on marital satisfaction (or in the husband's case on sexual fulfillment) represent the upper left-hand cell, the proportion in that cell will be higher than in the other cells on the subject of the ordination of women (above half) and lower than those in other cells in support of optional celibacy (less than half).

Yet in Tables 14.16 (page 193), this is precisely what occurs. The highest support for women priests and the strongest opposition to optional celibacy comes from those husbands and wives who have benefited (either in marital satisfaction in the wife's case or sexual fulfillment in the husband's) from a wife's confidant relationship with a priest.

The implications of this phenomenon for the social psychology and sociology of the celibate state are enormous. There is something in the "chemistry" of the relationship between a priest and a married woman which establishes an "electricity" often beneficial to both the wife and her husband and makes both of them more committed to celibacy and more committed to the ordination of women. The phenomenon ought to be studied in much greater detail but will doubtless be ignored. The left wing will not tolerate anything good to be said about celibacy and the right wing will not tolerate the thought that there is a special "chemistry" between the celibate and the married woman (and possibly between a celibate woman and a married man).

TABLE 14.16

Wife's Attitudes Towards Changes in the Clergy
by Confidant Status and Marital Satisfaction for Wives
(Percent)

	Marital Happiness	
Percent Pro Optional Celibacy:		
Has a Confidant	47	64
Has not	62	57
Percent Pro Women Priests:		
Has a Confidant	61	41
Has not	41	42

The Catholic Family in Transition

Highlights

1   *The American Catholic family is going through a transition period which seems, to some, to indicate an increase in divorce rates, intermarriages, single parent families, and working wives and mothers. More statistics show, however, that the divorce rate does not vary much by decade. Catholics seem to be only somewhat more likely to seek divorce, and no more likely to become involved in a mixed marriage than their non-Catholic counterparts.*

2   *There has been only a minor increase in the proportion of working mothers (Table 15.5)—probably the result of a decline in the number of children under six. The increase in working wives is not recent in American Catholicism and does not seem to be threatening the quality of the marital relationship (Table 15.6, 15.7).*

3   *There is an indication of problems with working mothers in their relationships to their daughters and to the religious development of their sons. (Table 15.12).*

4   *In ever increasing numbers American Catholics are rejecting the Church's teaching on birth control, divorce, and premarital sex while continuing to be overwhelmingly opposed to homosexuality and extramarital sex (Tables 15.4–15.17).*

Chapter 15

The Catholic Family in Transition

It is frequently alleged that the American Catholic family is currently going through a dramatic transition. Is this transition, in fact, occurring—and does it have some implications for the future development of religious imagination?

During the "year of the family" and the decade of the family, there has been considerable discussion of alleged changes in the Catholic family in the United States, many of them exciting, apparently irresistable trends that the Church must accept—trends allegedly affecting "old" and "new" families. Among the components of the change are, it is said, an increase in divorce rates (up to 40 percent), an increase in religious inter-marriages (up to 60 percent), an increase in number of single parent families, and an increase in working wives and mothers.

Doubtless there have been changes in the Catholic family in recent years, particularly in family size expectations, though even this change is in part a return to earlier average expectations. While there is considerable import for population increase over decline in expectations from 3.5 children to 2.8, such a change need not reflect a revolutionary change in values. Many of the other changes, however, are the result of assuming there was a time in the unspecified past when there was a golden age from which the present family is a deterioration or, perhaps, a liberation.

Examining these descriptions against the data in NORC's *General Social Survey* (Tables 15.1—15.3, pages 198 — 199), one discovers a somewhat less hellenic picture. Only 7 percent of Catholic adults are single marrieds. The mixed-marriage rates of each decade of age from twenty to seventy is approximately 30 percent—though in those marriages over thirty, there were enough conversions at the time of marriage to reduce the rate to 20 percent. The "ever-divorced" rate is 17 percent and does not vary much up or down by decade of age. There was a change in the ever-divorced Catholic proportion during the 1970s from 16 percent in the beginning of the decade to 18 percent at the end of the decade—a change concentrated almost entirely in Hispanic and poor segments of the population, probably as a result of the availability of free or inexpensive legal advice to deserted women in those segments of the population. Catholics then seem to be only marginally more likely to seek divorce and no more likely to seek as a spouse someone from another denomination. These statistics are so at odds with the conventional wisdom among many Catholic family-life "experts" that I have often been asked how NORC's data can be in such variance with the data of the known "experts." The only answer I can provide is that NORC's data is based on large national surveys professionally designed and collected, and statistically valid.

TABLE 15.1

Mixed Marriage Catholic Family by Age Cohort

		Percent Non-Catholic Spouse	Percent Spouse Raised Non-Catholic
20's	(331)	32	34
30's	(384)	23	29
40's	(208)	21	32
50's	(264)	14	29
60's	(159)	16	26
70's	(58)	17	12
80's	(10)	10	10
Total	(1514)	21	29

TABLE 15.2

Divorced and Single Parent Families by Sex for Catholics by Age Cohort

	Percent Ever Divorced		Percent Single Parent Families *	
	Men	Women	Men	Women
20's	13	16	4	9
30's	17	18	3	12
40's	22	21	8	11
50's	16	17	6	7
60's	18	19	4	6
70's	13	11	2	1
80's	0	5	0	0
Total	17	17	5	8

* This statistic is the result of the description of the number of children of men and women who are currently divorced or separated. It does not indicate which parent has the custody of the children.

TABLE 15.3

Family Size for Catholic Married Women
by Age Cohort

		Actual Number of Children	Expected Number of Children	Ideal Number of Children
20's	(451)	1.28	2.42	2.90
30's	(512)	2.74	3.00	2.96
40's	(433)	3.38	3.50	3.42
50's	(409)	2.90	2.90	3.50
60's	(279)	2.46	2.46	3.25
70's	(142)	2.73	2.73	3.40
80's	(37)	2.73	2.73	3.53
Total	(2300)	2.56	2.94	3.20

Thirty-six percent of the married women in their twenties work (Table 15.4, page 200), 29 percent of those in their thirties work, 48 percent of those in their forties work, and 44 percent of those in their fifties work. A quarter of the mothers in their twenties work, a little more than a third of those in their thirties work, and almost half of those in their forties work. Such proportions of working women and working mothers are clearly different from an era when mothers did not work. One must ask, however, when, if ever, that era existed. It was not during the rural proletarian time of the nineteenth century or before migration to the United States when women worked very hard indeed on the farm. Nor was it during the immigrant experience when women worked as maids, secretaries, and school teachers, often when their husbands could not find employment. Nor was it true in the Depression years when anyone in the family who could find work did—nor in the war industries of the 1940s. Nor did it seem to be true in the case of the 50s and the 60s, when the young adults in our Catholic study were growing up (Table 15.8, page 201), since 42 percent of the respondents in the young adult study said their mothers worked during at least two of the three periods about which they were questioned. Among these young adults, 31 percent reported that their mothers worked before they went to first grade, 51 percent reported that their mothers worked during grammar school, and 59 percent reported that their mothers worked while they were in high school. These high proportions were true even in young adults in their late twenties, who are therefore describing family situations which existed in the late 1940s and early 1950s. There has been a 4 percentage point increase in the proportion of working mothers in the 1970s (Table 15.5, page 200), hardly a revolutionary change and probably the result of a decline in the number of children under six.

TABLE 15.4

Working Wives by Age Cohort
(Percent)

| | Working Wives | | | Working Mothers (with husbands present) | | |
	Full Time	Part Time	Total	Full Time	Part Time	Total
20's	28	8	36	16	9	25
30's	23	16	39	21	16	37
40's	27	21	48	25	22	47
50's	30	14	44	26	16	42
60's	14	6	20	14	4	18

TABLE 15.5

Changing Patterns of Working Wives and Working Mothers for Catholic Women During the 1970's
(Percent)

| | Working Wives | | | Working Mothers | | |
	Full Time	Part Time	Total	Full Time	Part Time	Total
1974	23	11	34	21	12	33
1976	26	15	41	20	17	37
1978	27	14	41	22	15	37

Nor does a wife working seem to interfere with marital happiness or family happiness, either for the husband or for the wife (Tables 15.6 and 15.7, page 201). Thus, the increase in working wives is not recent in American Catholicism and does not seem to be threatening the quality of marital relationships. It may, however, have some negative impact on the parent/child relationship. Young men from families in which their mothers worked are somewhat less likely to be devout than those from families where mothers did not work (Table 15.9, page 202). Young women from such families are less likely to report that their childhood was very happy at least if the mother worked in all three periods. Furthermore, both groups, but especially the young women, are more likely to say that the parents' relationship with each other was very close. Husbands and wives today do not demonstrate any impact of a working wife on marital satisfaction. However, young people who grew up not so long ago seem to have perceived a negative impact on marital satisfaction, particularly if the mother worked in all three periods. Furthermore, (Table 15.12, page 203), if a mother worked in all three periods, it seems to have had a negative impact on the daughter's closeness to her mother. The implications of this finding for the religious imagination do not seem to be very great since the religious imagination is relatively less affected either by the happiness or by the closeness of daughter to mother, but it does hint that there are problems with working mothers particularly in their relationships to their daughters and the religious development of their sons which ought to be seriously considered.

TABLE 15.6

Marital Happiness by Working Wife
(Z score on scale combining marital and family happiness)

Wife		Husband	
Wife Working	Wife Not Working	Wife Working	Wife Not Working
−.01	.01	−.01	.01

TABLE 15.7

Personal Happiness by Working Wife
(Percent Very Happy)

Wife		Husband	
Wife Working	Wife Not Working	Wife Working	Wife Not Working
35	36	34	36

TABLE 15.8

Working Mothers of Young People by Age of Young People
(Percent of mothers who worked at least two of the periods: infancy, grammar school, high school)

13−17	57
18−20	47
21−23	43
24−27	44
28−30	42

As we see in Table 15.13 (page 204), however, the young people who have grown up in families with working mothers are the least likely to think that a child would be harmed if the mother works. Only 27 percent and 23 percent of the young men whose mothers worked during all three periods strongly agree that the child will be harmed—as opposed to 47 percent of the young men and 34 percent of the young women whose mothers did not work. Either the harm to the relationship between mother and daughter is spiritual harm not noticed by the children or is not considered important on some fundamental level. It may not represent serious harm. It also may be that the young people are, to some extent, deceiving themselves. One concludes, therefore, that while the increase in the proportion of working mothers is not recent in American Catholicism, it does not represent disaster for the family. It does imply certain problems and difficulties, particularly in a mother's relationship with her daughter and the son's religious development. It must be faced honestly or at least investigated more carefully.

TABLE 15.9

Religious Devotion of Children of Working Mothers by Sex (Knights of Columbus Study)

(Percent high on sacramental scale—Mass, communion and prayer)

Number of Times Mother Worked*	Men	Women
0	36	41
	N = (165)	(179)
1	32	37
	N = (136)	(174)
2	25	36
	N = (144)	(154)
3	22	38
	N = (107)	(106)

* Infancy, grammar school years, high school years. A score of three indicates a mother worked all of these times.

TABLE 15.10

Childhood Happiness by Working Mother by Sex

(Percent childhood was very happy)

Number of Times Mother Worked	Men	Women
0	36	44
1	33	42
2	34	39
3	32	26

The structures of Catholic family life have not changed very much despite loudly-offered opinions of the experts. However (Tables 15.14—15.17, pages 204—205), there has been tremendous change in Catholic sexual attitudes in the last twenty years. In 1963, about half the Catholic population thought contraception was wrong, 46 percent thought divorce was wrong, and 75 percent thought that premarital sex was wrong. By 1974, these proportions changed to 13 percent, 25 percent, and 35 percent, respectively. Only a quarter of the weekly communicants in 1974 rejected contraception, only a half rejected divorce, and only half rejected premarital sex. The change among young people in their twenties between 1963 and 1979 is even more striking. In 1963, 49 percent rejected contraception; in 1979 only 4 percent. In 1963, 41 percent rejected divorce; in 1979, 11 percent thought it was wrong. Seventy percent disapproved of premarital sex in 1963; fifteen years later only 17 percent disapproved of it. Virtually 80 percent of the weekly communicants who were Catholics in their twenties in 1963 disapproved of all three forms of sexual behavior. Now 13 percent of the weekly communicants in their twenties disapprove of contraception, 18 percent disapprove of divorce, and 34 percent disapprove of premarital sex.

TABLE 15.11

Parents' Relationship with Each Other by Working Mother as Evaluated by Young Men and Young Women

(Percent parents related "very well" to each other)

Number of Times Mother Worked	Men	Women
0	43	42
1	34	33
2	32	32
3	32	26

TABLE 15.12

Relationship Between Respondent and Mother When Growing Up by Working Mother by Sex

(Percent very close)

Number of Times Mother Worked	Men	Women
0	37	38
1	34	43
2	31	35
3	38	27

Returning to the GSS, we note a continued decline among Catholics of all ages during the 1970s in attitude toward premarital sex if not towards extramarital sex or homosexuality. In 1974, 32 percent of the men disapproved of premarital sex. By 1978, this had fallen to 22 percent. During the same period of time, the proportion disapproving of premarital sex for women (like the men of all ages) declined from 36 percent to 29 percent. There were, however, no comparable changes in approval of homosexuality or extramarital sex. The men were 6 percentage points more likely to approve of premarital sex in 1978 and 6 percentage points more likely to approve of homosexuality. Nonetheless, three-fifths of the men opposed extramarital sex in 1978 and seven-tenths of them opposed homosexuality.

TABLE 15.13

Attitudes Towards Working Mothers by Whether Young Person Had a Working Mother by Sex

(Percent thinking the child will be harmed)
(strongly agree or agree)

Number of Times Mother Worked	Men	Women
0	47	34
1	45	39
2	27	39
3	27	23

TABLE 15.14

A. CHANGING CATHOLIC SEXUAL VALUES
(Catholic School Studies)
(Percent)

	1963	1974
Contraception wrong	52	13
Divorce wrong	46	25
Premarital sex wrong	75	35

B. FOR WEEKLY COMMUNICANTS
(Percent)

	1963	1974
Contraception wrong	82	24
Divorce wrong	80	46
Premarital sex wrong	87	48

The decline in opposition to premarital sex occurred even among those who were weekly church attenders (Table 15.17). In the early 70s, 46 percent of this devout group disapproved of premarital sex. By late in the 1970's, this proportion had fallen to 28 percent. In the late 70s, in other words, a majority of even the most devout Catholics of all ages did not object at least in principle to premarital sexuality.

TABLE 15.15

A. CHANGING CATHOLIC SEXUAL ATTITUDES FOR THOSE IN THEIR TWENTIES
(Catholic School Studies, Young Adult Study)
(Percent)

	1963	1974	1979
Contraception wrong	49	7	4
Divorce wrong	41	17	11
Premarital sex wrong	70	35	17

B. FOR THOSE IN THEIR TWENTIES WHO ARE WEEKLY COMMUNICANTS
(Percent)

	1963	1974	1979
Contraception wrong	80	24	13
Divorce wrong	79	29	18
Premarital sex wrong	83	69	34

TABLE 15.16

Changing Catholic Sexual Attitudes in the 1970's
(Percent)

	Premarital Sex (wrong)		Extramarital Sex (wrong)		Homosexuality (wrong)	
	Men	Women	Men	Women	Men	Women
1974	32	36	67	78	76	67
1976	24	31	62	72	66	64
1978	22	29	61	72	70	67

TABLE 15.17

Premarital Sex Wrong for Weekly Church Attenders
(Men and women together)
(Percent)

1974	46
1976	38
1978	38

To report these findings is not necessarily to approve of them. However, any honest consideration of the Catholic family must note that in ever-increasing numbers, American Catholics reject the Church's teaching on birth control, divorce, premarital sex, and judging by the 1980 GSS figures, the Pope's visit to America and his stern attempts to impose more "order and discipline" on Catholic practice in the United States had no effect whatsoever on these attitudes. Catholics continue to be overwhelmingly opposed to homosexuality and extramarital sex. But sexual behaviors which as recently as twenty years ago were disapproved by high majorities of Catholics are now no longer viewed with great disfavor. The structures of Catholic family life have not changed as the Catholic marriage education "experts" so loudly complain, but Catholic attitudes on certain aspects of sexuality, such as birth control and premarital sex, have undergone an enormous change. To pretend otherwise would be dishonest and self-deceptive. The major changes, however, in the ambiance of American Catholic family life (and the life of families of whatever religion) are rarely noted by the marriage education "experts."

What then is the condition of the Catholic family? One must be profoundly skeptical about pronouncements by those who claim to be specialists in family life. Tolerance for the working mother, for premarital liaisons, and for decrease of the number of children are all phenomena which are certainly taking place, though they do not necessarily represent anything that has not been experienced previously in the history of the Catholic family. Grave concern about an increase in Catholic divorce, religious inter-marriage, and single parent rates simply are not supported by the data. Working mothers are indeed a substantial proportion of the Catholic population but they do not represent a new phenomenon. And while working mothers do seem to increase certain family problems, they scarcely represent a disastrous structural change for Catholic family life. While there have been immense changes in Catholic attitudes toward certain kinds of sexual behavior in the last twenty years, these changes do not indicate a blanket approval of "permissiveness" or "promiscuity."

The family, as noted previously, is a highly flexible and dynamic institution always undergoing change though usually within the broad constraints of cultural tradition. It is important for the Catholic Church, if it intends to continue to minister to families (and presumably it will do so), to be sensitive to these changes and seek to understand them. Such sensitivity would presuppose, however, the quest for accurate, precise information as well as a certain skepticism about proclamations of dramatic "revolutions."

The Womanliness of God

Highlights

1 *Men need the image of God-as-woman more than women do. Men who have a womanly image of God will find it easier to think of God as a lover, will pray more often and more intensely, and will be more committed to the social concerns which come from a deep religious devotion (Table 16.1).*

2 *Men who have a womanly image of God seem to have better relationships with women, more fulfilling sexual experiences in marriage, and be more likely to say they were very close to their mother, and have "warm" images of Mary (Table 16.1).*

3 *Men who say their mothers had a strong impact on their religious development are almost three times as likely to report that they imagine God as mother as those who do not report such maternal influence.*

4 *Men who say that their wives have a powerful impact on their religious development are more than three times as likely as other men to imagine God as mother (Table 16.2).*

5 *Woman seem to reveal the feminine dimension of God to men.*

Chapter 16

The Womanliness of God

I will contend in this chapter that men need the image of God-as-woman more than women do.

The most striking image of the womanliness of God in recent years was presented in Bob Fosse's film *All That Jazz* described in the opening chapter of this book. It is, as we have said, the story of Fosse's brush with death during a massive heart attack. The death experience, however, turned out to be an interlude of grace. Death itself seemed to be very much like a woman—a tender, sensuous lover who sees through the phoniness of Joe Gideon (the fictional Fosse) and loves him anyway. Indeed, Angelique (Jessica Lange, King Kong's sometime girl friend) is a summation of all the women in Gideon's life. She gently wipes the sweat from his hands as he is dying as would his wife, threatens to absorb him with a passionate kiss at the very end as have his mistresses, and playfully mocks him as does his daughter (indeed in the final sequence the identification between Angelique and his daughter is heavily emphasized—the daughter's tears make Angelique sad).

Demanding, sexy, a bit sinister, inescapable, tender, and passionately loving—that's what the angel of death is like, Fosse tells us. The angel may also be God. Fosse is not sure, yet twice in the movie he brackets scenes with Ms. Lange in references to God; and at the end he gives us a choice: either life ends with a lifeless corpse being zipped up in a plastic bag or in the consummation of a love affair with a beautiful spouse.

According to *All That Jazz* then, death is a beautiful woman, and the beautiful woman may be God. Fosse doesn't insist. Like any good poet he merely suggests . . . yet what if he's right?

It seemed to me as I reflected on the film that in principle we men ought to have more invested in the image of God as someone like Jessica Lange than women might. God, we are told, is love. Our relationship to God is a love relationship. Normally, the most powerful love experiences we have are cross-sexual relationships. It is hard to fit these experiences into an imagery of God which is predominately male.

The usual reaction (even with college students, I find) to a comparison of human love with divine love is to insist that it is utterly different from sexual attraction ("not at all physical," my students tell me). Thus, to use scholastic terms, the word "love" is predicated equivocally of intimacy with humans and intimacy with God.

I do not believe, however, that such an equivocal predication will stand the test of either good spirituality or good exegesis. If love with God isn't really like human love at all, then it can hardly be very appealing, since human love is the most powerful emotion of which we are capable. Moreover, the sexual imagery of the Scriptures is washed away if the usage is equivocal.

Thus we must conclude that the use of "love" is analogous. God does passionately desire us in a way similar to how an attractive member of the opposite sex might desire us. And we desire God in a way similar to the way we might desire an appealing member of the opposite sex. (I trust I will be excused in this book from discussing images for Gays. While the subject is proper and important, it is beyond the goals of this preliminary essay.)

Of any analogy one must inquire how the two uses differ. There can be only one answer: divine love is more passionate than human love. God's desire for us is greater than that of any human spouse; and God's appeal is more powerful than that of any human bedmate. God is different from Jessica Lange mainly in that God is more attractive, more demanding, more tender, more passionate, more gentle.

If there is any validity in these reflections it would follow that men who have a womanly image of God will find it easier to think of God as a lover, will pray more often and more intensely, and will be more deeply committed to the social concerns which should come from intense religious devotion. Moreover, precisely because they are involved in a love relationship with a womanly God, they should have better relationships with human women. Finally, it seems not unlikely that their womanly image of God will be affected by their relationships with their mother and by strong, womanly images of Mary.

These predictions would substantiate my "theory" only if they did not also apply, or at least did not apply to such a great extent, to women's imagery of God-as-woman.

It is possible to test these hypotheses against data collected in the Knights of Columbus' study of young Catholics. All the hypotheses are sustained.

Some 10 percent of young American Catholics say that they are extremely likely to imagine God as a "mother." There are no differences between young men and young women in this proportion. However (Table 16.1), men with a womanly image of God are significantly more likely than men who do not have that image also to imagine God as a lover, to pray often, to offer prayers of gratitude, to consider a life of social concern and involvement to be important, to say that their sexual fulfillment in marriage is excellent, and to be in marriages in which both husband and wife report the sexual fulfillment excellent. They also are more likely to say they were very close to their mother and to score high on a scale which measures their image of Mary as "patient" and "comforting." In only two of the variables are there significant relationships in the same direction for women—the image of God as lover and closeness to mother.

TABLE 16.1

Correlates of God as Mother for Men and Women
(Percent)

	Men GOD AS MOTHER		Women GOD AS MOTHER	
	"Extremely Likely"	Not "Extremely Likely"	"Extremely Likely"	Not "Extremely Likely"
God as Lover (extremely likely)	76*	22	57*	25
Prayer (several times a week at least)	63*	42	61	65
Prayers of Gratitude (often)	64*	46	60	60
Own Sexual Fulfillment "Excellent"	80*	38	38	47
Both husband and wife say sexual fulfillment "Excellent"	33*	22	15	27*
Social concerns "Extremely Important"	43*	21	21	25
Was very close to mother	42*	32	52*	31
High on Mary scale ("Patient" and "Comforting" both "Extremely likely" as image)	78*	58	77	75

* Differences statistically significant.

Women who think of God as a mother are twice as likely to think of God also as a lover than those who do not imagine God as mother, but men with the picture of God as mother are three times more likely to imagine her also as a lover than are men without that picture.

They are also half again as likely to be in marriages in which both they and their wives say the sexual fulfillment is excellent. Picturing God as a mother is not only good for the prayer life of a man, it is also good for the sex life of his wife.

So the Fosse/Gideon experience of the womanliness of God is not as rare as one might have thought. While a tenth of the Catholic men under thirty is surely a minority, it is by no means a trivial number of young men who imagine God as a mother and who are likely to benefit in their spiritual and sexual lives from that image.

One is forced to wonder where the image comes from; surely it does not originate in any educational or spiritual direction experiences they have had. Perhaps it results from experiences with women in which they sense that God has disclosed herself to them.

Confirmation of this explanation can be found in the data. Men who say their mothers had a strong impact on their religious development are almost three times as likely to report that they imagine God as mother as do those who do not report such maternal influence. Furthermore, men who say that their wives have a powerful impact on their religious development are more than three times as likely as are other men to imagine God as mother (Table 16.2). There is no parallel effect on the religious imagery of women respondents.

TABLE 16.2

Influence of Women on a Man's Image of God-As-Woman
Percent "Extremely Likely" to Imagine God as Mother

	Men		Women	
	Powerful Effect	Not Powerful	Powerful Effect	Not Powerful
Mother	18	7	9	10
Spouse	18	5	13	10

Women, then, seem to mediate the womanliness of God for men. Apparently they do so without seeking permission from the magisterium. Religious imagery with its profound effect on human life and human religion is shaped with little attention to and little support from or awareness of the institutional Church.

The implications of these findings for spiritual and pastoral theology as well as for prayer and spiritual direction are enormous. They are also shattering and revolutionary. A woman may well imagine herself as a bride of Christ (and a married woman or an unmarried lay woman has as much right to that image as does a religious woman). But a man imagine himself as the husband of God? Or God as his paramour? Or God as a woman pursuing him with passionate desire? How shocking and scandalous. God may desire women but certainly not men.

Yet however scandalous and shocking the implications, the findings are hard to dispute. Some young men do benefit from cross-sexual images of God, and so do their spouses. And as we discovered in the last chapter, some young women do benefit from cross-sexual confidant relationships with priests. And so do their spouses.

It is too bad that the synod of bishops said the last word on human sexuality. Otherwise one might think that we were only beginning to understand the relationship between sex and religion, between sexual images and the life of the spirit.

In the meantime, I, for one, take consolation that God, when finally encountered, will be even more spectacular than Jessica Lange. She'd better be.

Hispanic and Canadian Stories

Highlights

1   *Certain qualifications must be noted with regard to the analysis of Spanish-American and French-Canadian families:*
    ●Canadian data is valid only for those between 14 and 30.
    ● Until a "sampling frame" is devised which takes into account the peculiar regional distribution of the Spanish-American population, all surveys are less adequate than the number of respondents normally would indicate.
    ● There is a lower response rate among Spanish Americans, possibly based perhaps on a general distrust of government agencies.

2   *Family values, family structures and economic situations differ widely but the dynamics which shape the religious imagination are the same among all four groups considered–Hispanic, non-Hispanic Americans, and English and French Canadians (Tables 17.11, 17.12).*

3   *The French Canadians are more likely to have a vivid and gracious religious imagination than the other groups; they are far more likely to think of God as mother and lover than the others (Table 17.10).*

4   *French Canadians are more "permissive" on all sexual items than are their English counterparts (Table 17.3).*

5   *The Spanish Americans, more traditional in their family culture, are less "permissive" in their sexual attitudes than are other Americans, but aside from this, the statistical differences are minimal (Table 17.3).*

6   *The processes which shape the religious imaginations of French Canadians and Spanish Americans–religious experience, sensitivity to nature, family, friends, and parish community–are the same in all four subcultures (Table 17.9).*

Chapter 17

Hispanic and Canadian Stories

Within every society there are subcultures which differ to a greater or lesser extent from the larger society. This chapter investigates the development of the religious imagination among Spanish Americans and, since data are available from the *Young Catholic Adult* study about Canadians, it investigates as well the religious imagination of French Canadians. Before analyzing the development of the religious imagination of these two subgroups, however, we present a brief description of the family structure of these two subcultures.

The consideration of both "bicultural" groups (again the word is used with no other than its denotive meaning) suffers certain handicaps. Our Canadian data are based entirely on the NORC/KC study of young adults and hence are valid only for those between 14 and 30. In the United States we also have some family material available in NORC's ongoing *General Social Survey*. In both surveys, however, the sampling "efficiency" for the Spanish is suspect because of the peculiar regional distribution of the Spanish-American population which is concentrated in certain parts of the country. Until a "sampling frame" is devised which takes into account this regional distribution, all surveys of Spanish-Americans are less adequate than the number of respondents would normally indicate. In addition, there seems to be a serious response rate problem among Spanish Americans, perhaps based on distrust of government agencies and indeed of anyone who asks questions (as a possible agent for the Immigration and Naturalization Service). These qualifications must be kept in mind as the present brief analysis proceeds.

Three major assumptions guided the course of the analysis:

1. The basic outline of problems and possibilities in the Western family described in the oral presentation transcends national, cultural, and linguistic boundaries.

2. Nonetheless, the Spanish and French family patterns may be somewhat more traditional than the "English speaking" family patterns (as an Irish American I resolutely refuse to describe myself or anyone else, save those who have a right to the titles, as either "Anglo" or "Yankee").

3. In addition, the Spanish-American family may well suffer some of the tribulations which come from being victims of poverty.

The first of the six tables considers the "family of origin"—the family in which our young adults grew up (Table 17.1). On all but one item (closeness to father), there is indeed a statistically significant difference between the Spanish and other Americans; and on four of the items, significant differences between the English and French Canadians (items concerning working mothers and closeness to the mother).

TABLE 17.1

	Spanish American	Other American	English Canadian	French Canadian
Family Growing Up (Percent)				
Did not grow up with both parents	24*	14	10	14
Mother and father were very close	25*	36	39	44
Mother and self very close	44*	35	33	44**
Father and self very close	20	22	19	23
Childhood was not happy	18*	11	13	11
Father made family decisions by self	24*	18	20	14
Father punished by self	18*	26	27	22
Mother worked while infant	42*	30	24	13**
Mother worked while child	58*	50	44	24**
Mother worked while teen	59*	58	52	37**

* Statistically different from non-Spanish Americans.
** Statistically different from English Canadians.

The economic deprivation of the Spanish shows its effect in the higher proportion which did not grow up with both parents, the lower proportion which say their parents were "very close" to one another, and the higher proportion reporting unhappy childhoods. In both the "more traditional" families, relationships with the mother were more likely to be warm than in the English-speaking families (we Irish Americans do speak English, after a fashion at any rate). The father was more likely to make the decisions by himself in the Spanish family but less likely to unilaterally impose punishments—a mixture of paternalism and non-paternalism which seems to fit the anthropological research on that culture. Finally, the French-Canadian family was more "traditional" in that the mothers of the young people were less likely to have worked during childhood, while the Spanish-American family was less traditional in that mothers, driven doubtless by economic necessity, were more likely to work than their English-speaking counterparts.

There are only two statistically significant differences in the newly formed families of procreation of our young adults (Table 17.2). French Canadians expect fewer children and Spanish Americans are less likely to be satisfied in their marriages (again, one suspects, for economic reasons: research shows that economic deprivation has a strong negative effect on marriage). It is worth noting that in all four groups about one-fifth of the young adults who are in "relationships" have either been divorced or are living together out of wedlock. The latter proportion may be a low estimate because it is not unlikely that many of those living in such relationships would not respond to our survey (though the response rate was 80 percent in both countries).

TABLE 17.2

Family Now				
	Spanish American	Other American	English Canadian	French Canadian
Percent divorced	10	9	8	6
Number of children expected	2.7	2.6	2.6	2.3**
Percent very happy in marriage	55*	65	73	64
Percent sexual fulfillment excellent	48	44	65	59

* Statistically different from non-Spanish Americans.
** Statistically different from English Canadians.

Save for the absence of difference between Spanish and non-Spanish Americans on abortion when there is fear of a defective child (and the abortion items measure the legal permissability, not the desirability of abortion), all the comparisons in Table 17.3 (page 220) are significant. As one would expect, the Spanish Americans, more traditional in their family culture, are also less "permissive" in their sexual attitudes than are other Americans. However, just the opposite is the case for the French Canadians who are on all items more "permissive" than their

English counterparts. Note that the French Canadians are almost twice as likely to see nothing wrong in premarital sex as are the Spanish Americans. More traditional in their past family structure, the French Canadians now seem more permissive in their sexual attitudes. The "big change" in the family about which so much has been said by some Catholics in the United States (mostly without data, be it noted) does indeed seem to have occurred in French Canada—perhaps with migration to the cities.

TABLE 17.3

Sexual and Marital Attitudes
(Percent)

	Spanish American	Other American	English Canadian	French Canadian
Birth control wrong	11*	5	8	2**
Premarital sex never wrong	43*	52	64	77**
Living together before marriage never wrong	46*	54	57	80**
Divorce not wrong	79*	90	78	90**
Would permit abortion if risk of defective child	82	82	73	85**
Would permit abortion if mother wants no more children	36*	43	40	40

* Statistically different from non-Spanish Americans.
** Statistically different from English Canadians.

French Canadians are relatively more traditional in their attitudes towards the role of women, more likely than their English opposites to fear harm to the child if the mother works, and less likely to support the ordination of women. Spanish Americans are more traditional than non-Spanish Americans in attitudes towards the importance of children and the danger of the working mother. (Working mothers is a more recent phenomenon in French Canada than it is in the United States, as we have seen in Table 17.1.)

Thus, both in past and present structures, behavior, and attitudes, there are traces of more "traditional" patterns in both the non-English speaking sub-cultures. The Spanish "tradition" is handicapped by the effects of poverty and the French tradition has apparently undergone a rapid change. Both are sufficiently different from the "majority" (English Catholics are the numerical minority) that one must take these differences into account in applying the general remarks about the "North Atlantic" family to their specific situations. On the other hand, the importance of the differences ought not to be exaggerated. More than four-fifths of the young people in all four groups reject the birth control teaching, for example. Half (or almost half) think there is nothing wrong with living together before marriage. More than two-fifths agree on the extreme importance of children for life happiness, and more than two-fifths support the ordination of women (though only among English Canadians—and Irish Catholic Americans—does that support go above 50 percent).

The next two tables (17.4, 17.5, page 222) turn to the NORC *General Social Survey* for a comparison of all adults over eighteen who are Spanish with those who are not Spanish. Again most of the differences are statistically significant and indicate the persistence of an older tradition among the Spaniards in their attitude towards the role of women. They also indicate a higher divorce rate and a desire for easier divorce laws, doubtless because of the economic pressures on Spanish-American family life (most of the increase in the proportion "ever divorced" during the 1970s has occurred in the poor segments of the population, in part, it is speculated, because of the availability of free legal advice and inexpensive divorces).

There is also evidence of a traditional double standard (Table 17.6, page 223) with the Hispanic Americans more tolerant of extramarital sex than their non-Spanish opposites. This difference, as the tradition of the double standard would lead us to expect, is to be found only among men.

Despite overarching similarities, there are differences among subcultural groups within the North Atlantic community (and there are other differences among the English-speaking American ethnic groups which are not touched on in this study—it suffices to say for the record that the Irish tradition of strong women does not seem to be diminishing). The two non-English speaking groups do show tendencies to keep alive certain more traditional attitudes and behaviors (though these differences are relative and within a context of fundamental similarities). The Spanish tradition is plagued by poverty and the French tradition seems to be undergoing a rapid change, the meaning of which, to say nothing about the response to which, we must leave to others. There are no correlations in either direction between having a mother who worked and attitudes towards mothers working for both English-speaking groups. However, in the two more traditional familial cultures, the more likely a person is to have come from a family with a working mother, the more sympathetic that person is to a woman working—and less likely to think that the children will be harmed. The experience of being raised by a working mother, in other words, disposes French-Canadian and Spanish-American respondents to approve of working mothers. This is not the case with the English-speaking groups, probably because they are not in a cultural transition and are less concerned about the impact of working mothers on children.

TABLE 17.4

"Feminist" Attitudes
(Percent)

	Spanish American	Other American	English Canadian	French Canadian
Ordination of women "important"	43	43	54	47**
If mother works, child likely to suffer harm	41*	35	40	57**
Children "extremely important" for life happiness	49*	39	42	40

* Statistically different from non-Spanish Americans.
** Statistically different from English Canadians.

TABLE 17.5

**Attitudes of American Catholic by Ethnic Background
(NORC General Social Survey—Adults Over 18)**
(Percent)

	Spanish (n = 229)	Other Catholics (n = 5690)
Women should take care of home, leave country to men	43*	31
Disapprove of woman earning money if husband can support her	44*	30
Would not vote for qualified woman for president	23*	17
Approve abortion (defect)	76*	81
Approve abortion (wants no more children)	35	33
Premarital sex never wrong	35	33
Extramarital sex never wrong or sometimes not wrong	18*	11
Change divorce laws (easier)	31*	26
Percent ever divorced	23*	16
Ideal number of children	3.25	3.17

* Statistically different from non-Spanish Americans.

Only some of the potential negative effects of working mothers discussed in a previous chapter seem to affect the Spanish-American family. If the mother worked during all three periods of a young person's life, it does seem to be a negative effect on the religious devotion of the young person and on the young person's closeness to the mother (Table 17.7). However, the mother's working affected neither the happiness of the childhood nor the young person's perception of whether the parents related well. The impact on closeness to mother on Spanish Americans (Table 17.8, page 224) was stronger for men than for women while the reverse was true (as we remember from a previous chapter) for the non-Spanish. The negative impact of a working mother on religious devotion was especially strong for Spanish-American young men. The Spanish-American family, therefore, copes relatively well with the economic necessity that forces mothers to work against the demands of the culture save but the fact that young Spanish-American men are even more negatively affected in their closeness to their mother by having a working mother than are young American women, either Spanish or non-Spanish.

TABLE 17.6

Attitudes Towards Extramarital Sex for Men and Women in the United States (General Social Survey)
(Percent)

	Percent Never Wrong or Sometimes Not Wrong	
	Spanish	Non-Spanish
Men	23*	18
Women	13	14

* Significantly different from non-Spanish.

TABLE 17.7

Effects of Working Mothers on Spanish American Young People
(Percent)

Working Mother	High on Sacramental Scale		Happy Youth		Parents Related Very Well		Very Close to Mother	
	Spanish	Non-Spanish	Spanish	Non-Spanish	Spanish	Non-Spanish	Spanish	Non-Spanish
0	31	39	27	42	20	43	65	36
1	19	39	27	39	36	34	35	39
2	29	30	30	36	17	34	44	32
3	21	29	33	30	27	29	32	32

The "stories of God" in the religious imagination of young Spanish Americans (Table 17.9, page 224) is virtually the same as that of their non-Spanish counterparts, although the latter are somewhat

likely to check all eight "warm" adjectives in their
riptions of Jesus and Mary. Furthermore, the same dynamics
which shape the religious imaginations of the young non-Spanish
Catholic also shape the religious imagination of the Spanish
Catholic with religious experience having a somewhat more
powerful impact and sermons having a somewhat less powerful
impact on the religious imagination of the young Hispanic
American. But considerable cultural differences between the two
groups of American Catholics do not prevent them from having
basically similar religious imaginations which are shaped by
basically similar dynamic systems.

TABLE 17.8

Correlations for Hispanics Between Working Wives and Family Structure
(Coefficient of Correlation = Pearson's r)

	Spanish		Non-Spanish	
	Men	Women	Men	Women
Happy childhood	.11	.04	.04	−.12
Parents related well	−.05	−.03	−.11	−.14
Close to mother	−.18	−.10	−.03	−.14
Sacramental scale	−.18	−.07	−.06	−.05

TABLE 17.9

Stories of God for Spanish Americans
(Percent)

	Spanish	Non-Spanish
"Grace" (percent top one-fourth)	20	21
"God/Heaven" (percent top one-fourth)	21	20
"Jesus/Mary" (percent all eight adjectives)	26	43

However, the two Canadian subcultures do differ considerably in
their religious imagination (Table 17.10, page 225). While there is
no difference in the images of Jesus and Mary between the English
and French Canadians, there are substantial and statistically
significant differences between the two Canadian subcultures in
both the God/heaven scale and in the grace scale—16 percentage
points more likely to be high on the former and 15 percentage
points more likely to be high on the latter. French Canadians, in
other words, are far more likely to think of God as a father and a
mother and heaven as an action-filled paradise of pleasure and
delight than their English-Canadian counterparts.

TABLE 17.10

Stories of God for English and French Canadians
(Percent)

	English	French
Grace (top two-fifths)	32	47*
God/Heaven (top one-third)	19	35*
Jesus/Mary (all eight adjectives)	40	40

* Difference statistically significant.

TABLE 17.11

Correlations With Grace Scale for Canadians
(Coefficient of Correlation = Pearson's r)

	English	French
Experience	.13	.19
Nature	.13	.06
Family	.12	.20
Friends	.18	.11
Sermons	.13	.18

TABLE 17.12

Standardized Correlations With Grace Scale for Canadians
(Betas)

	English	French
Experience	.07	.19
Nature	.07	.06
Family	.06	.20
Friends	.17	.11
Sermons	.14	.18
R =	.27	.32
R² =	.07	.11

The same "layered" set of dynamics, however, influences the religious imagination of both the English and French Canadians, (Tables 17.11; 17.12). With family and religious experiences being more important for the French Canadians and friends being somewhat more important for the English Canadians, the outcomes may be different but the processes and dynamics are the same.

Despite different sets of family values and family structures and despite economic differences, the dynamics which shape the religious imagination are the same among all four cultural groups being considered—Hispanic and non-Hispanic Americans, and English and French Canadians. The French Canadians are more likely to have a vivid and gracious religious imagination than the other groups especially because they are far more likely to think of God as a mother and a lover than are English Canadians and both American groups. The processes shaping their religious imaginations—religious experience, sensitivity to nature, family, friends, and parish community—are the same in all four subcultures. We can thus assert with considerable confidence that the model presented at the beginning of the book to explain the development of religious imagination has considerable validity for it applies in four different subcultural environments. In the next chapter we will attempt to determine whether it also applies to those who are not Catholic.

Those Who Are Not Catholic

Highlights

1   *Those respondents who are not Catholics are those persons who were married to Catholics completing the survey. The profiles (Tables 18.2, 18.3, and 18.4) cannot be taken to be representative of the profile of the religious imagination of all non-Catholic Americans.*

2   *The fundamental similarity in the religious imagination of the two groups is striking. There is virtually no difference between either group in their images of God as mother and lover, of Jesus as warm and reassuring, and of heaven as pleasure-filled and active (Table 18.5).*

3   *The dynamic which affects the religious imagination of the two groups is also similar (Table 18.6).*

4   *Not only is the religious imagination of the non-Catholics shaped by forces similar to those which shaped the Catholic religious imagination, it also seems to have a similarity on religious values and devotions.*

5   *Since there are many similarities found among those respondents who were Catholic and those who were not Catholic, it may mean that this common revelation of loving goodness and hope-renewing experiences is truly the work of the Holy Spirit. Rather than being a cause for alarm, it should be a cause for great rejoicing at the developments on ecumenism today.*

Chapter 18

Those Who Are Not Catholic

The funding agency sponsoring the study was interested in the problems of Catholic youth and hence there were no non-Catholics in the primary sample. However, questionnaires were administered to the spouses of those Catholic respondents who were married. Since some of those spouses were not Catholic, we do have information on the religious imagination of those "non-Catholics" who are married to Catholics. (There is not an adequate substitute for the term "non-Catholic." Its use here is intended to be neutral.)

A third of those respondents who are still Catholic and 94 percent of those who are no longer Catholic are married to members of other religious denominations or to those who have no religious affiliation at all. Of those who are no longer Catholic, 41 percent are married to those who have no religious affiliation, and another 19 percent to respondents who have "other" religious affiliation. Fifteen percent of those who are still Catholics are also married to "others" or "nones." One percent of these who are still Catholics are married to Jews and 3 percent to those who have disaffiliated from the Church. Nineteen percent of those who are still Catholics, 29 percent of those who have left the Church are married to Protestants (Table 18.1, page 230).

How does the religious imagination of those whose spouses are not Catholic compare to the religious imagination of those who married Catholics in our sample?

First of all, there are relatively few differences between the two groups in their imagery of God (Table 18.2, page 230). The profile for a non-Catholic is slightly to the left of the profile for Catholics; that is to say, non-Catholics are less likely to endorse any of these other categories. However, the differences are not great. Perhaps, imagery of the deity is part of the general American religious culture and is not affected by denominational affiliation.

Furthermore (Table 18.3, page 231), Catholics are somewhat more likely to think of Jesus as gentle, warm, patient, and comforting than the non-Catholics. There are no other major differences in the imagery of Jesus between the two groups. However, as might be expected, Catholics have a consistently more benign image of Mary than do non-Catholics, although one could hardly say on the basis of Table 18.3 that there was hostility to Mary among our non-Catholic respondents.

TABLE 18.1

Spouse's Religion by Whether Respondent Is Still Catholic
(Percent)

	Respondent Still Catholic	Respondent No Longer Catholic
Spouse		
Catholic	65	6
Jewish	1	3
Baptist	4	8
Methodist	5	8
Presbyterian	4	0
Lutheran	5	8
Episcopalian	1	5
Other	6	19
None	9	41
Total	100 (358)	100 (97) (N)

TABLE 18.2

Images of God for Non-Catholics and Catholics
(Mean Score[*])

	Catholics [a]	Non Catholics
Judge	2.20	2.25
Protector	1.61	1.83
Redeemer	1.80	1.94
Lover	2.66	2.83
Master	2.03	2.13
Mother	3.23	3.34
Creator	1.36	1.50
Father	1.70	1.97

[a] The Catholics are all married respondents. N = 415
The non-Catholics are all married to Catholics. N = 170
[*] The lower the score, the more likely the religious image.

Finally (Table 18.4, page 231), the imagery of the hereafter among both groups is basically similar, though Catholics are a little more likely to think of heaven as a paradise of pleasure and delight.

There is no reason to believe that those Americans who are not Catholics who elect to marry Catholic spouses are representative of the rest of the American non-Catholic population. Furthermore, as we have noted previously, spouses affect one another's religious imagination. Therefore, the profiles presented in Tables 18.2, 18.3, and 18.4 should not be taken to be representative of the profile of the religious imagination of all Americans who are not Catholic.

TABLE 18.3

Images of Jesus and Mary for Non-Catholics and Catholics
(Mean Score)

| | Jesus | | Mary | |
	Catholics	Non Catholics	Catholics	Non Catholics
Gentle	1.32	1.50	1.25	1.56
Stern	2.41	2.42	3.09	3.18
Warm	1.35	1.54	1.31	1.64
Distant	3.12	3.09	3.23	3.06
Demanding	2.76	2.65	3.36	3.29
Patient	1.35	1.53	1.36	1.78
Irrelevant	3.48	3.33	3.42	3.15
Challenging	2.44	2.54	3.08	3.22
Comforting	1.41	1.58	1.43	1.83

TABLE 18.4

Images of the After Life for Non-Catholics and Catholics
(Mean Score)

	Catholics	Non Catholics
Tranquility	1.52	1.55
Action	2.96	2.98
Similar Life	2.39	2.45
Loss of this life	2.75	2.61
Shadow	3.32	3.26
Spiritual Life	2.00	1.81
Paradise of Delight	2.48	2.61
Intellectual Communion with God	1.92	2.00
Union with God	1.43	1.51
Reunion with Loved Ones	1.50	1.66

Nevertheless, the fundamental similarity in the religious imagination of the two groups is striking. As can be observed in the percentages in Table 18.5 (page 232), there is virtually no difference between the two groups in the picture of God as a mother and a lover, of Jesus as warm and reassuring, and of heaven as an action-filled paradise of pleasure and delight. Only on the Mary scale are Catholics substantially higher than non-Catholics, and it is this difference that accounts for their different scores on the summary "grace" scale. Nevertheless, while three-fifths of the Catholics in the country have a "warm" image of Mary (describing her as extremely likely to be warm, patient, comforting, and gentle), so do two-fifths of the non-Catholics (and more than half of the Protestants in the sample). Whatever doctrinal difference may separate their religious denominations on the subject of the Madonna, there is much less difference between Catholics and non-Catholics on the imagery of Mary.

TABLE 18.5

Religious Imagination of Non-Catholics (Percent)			
	"Grace"	God/Mother/Lover (upper third)	Heaven
Catholics	40	32	31
Non-Catholics	22	32	28
	Jesus	Mary (four adjectives)	
Catholics	51	63	
Non-Catholics	48	39	

Not only is there a basic similarity in the religious imagination of the two groups, but the dynamic which affects the religious imagination seems to be similar. There are not enough non-Catholic spouses in the sample to create a path diagram that was produced for Catholics in previous chapters. But it is possible to determine how a scale of the five forces (family, nature, religious experience, friends, and the quality of parish life) which seem to influence the religious imagination affects Catholics and non-Catholics. In Table 18.6 (page 233) we see that the correlation between the grace scale and a scale made up of these five ("grace shaping") dynamisms for both Catholics and non-Catholics is quite similar (.27 for Catholics and .20 for non-Catholics).

Finally, not only is the religious imagination of the non-Catholics shaped by forces similar to those which shaped the Catholic religious imagination, it also seems to have a similarity to religious values and devotions. While there is no significant relationship between the grace scale and church attendance for our non-Catholic respondents, there is a .23 correlation with frequent prayer, and a .37 correlation with a hopeful response to tragedy—virtually the same coefficients that were presented for our Catholic respondents in Chapter 3. To the extent that our non-Catholic respondents may represent the religious imagination of all Americans who are not Catholic, it may be said that with the exception of the Mary image, the religious imagination of non-Catholics is similar to that of Catholics, is shaped by the same dynamisms, and has the same religious effect (Table 18.7).

TABLE 18.6

Correlation Between Variables Predicting Religious Imagination for Catholics and Non-Catholics

(Coefficient of Correlation = Pearson's r)

Catholics	Non-Catholics
.27	.20

TABLE 18.7

Correlations Between Religious Values and Behavior and "Grace" Scale for Non-Catholics

(Coefficient of Correlation = Pearson's r)

Church Attendance	Frequent Prayer	Hope
.07*	.23	.37

* Not significant.

There are three different possible responses to this finding. The humanists will rejoice, perhaps, at the thought that there is a basic similarity in the religious imagination of all Americans, which reveals some fundamental, underlying religious unity. Conservative Catholics may be dismayed that young Catholics are "not any different at all" in their religious imagination than young non-Catholics (save in their warm images of Mary). Historians of culture may respond by saying that after two thousand years of Christian history, certain basic religious images might be culture-wide, regardless of denominational affiliation (with some variations across subcultures such as the higher propensity of French-Canadian Catholics to think of God as a mother and a lover). Or one might say that God's Spirit (should there be one) is likely to blow "whither He will" (to quote Jesus' words) and that the revelation of loving goodness in hope-renewing experiences is not necessarily tied to denominational structures.

Chapter 19

Rediscovering the Story

In social science no theory is ever proved. The most one can say is that it has not been disproved. Propositions derived from a theory which views religion as originating in experiences of hope that are encoded in stories retained in the imagination are not falsified by the empirical evidence. The religious imagination, as described by admittedly crude measures, relates more powerfully to religious attitudes and behavior than does doctrinal orthodoxy. The religious imagination is shaped, in substantial part, by experiences of loving grace, particularly relational experiences with family, friends, teachers, clergymen, and especially one's spouse. Our theory, then, has considerable utility in both explaining the origins of the religious imagination and in predicting its impact.

Two objections are sometimes voiced when I discuss this research. The first is quite explicit: Does not the theory reduce religion to emotions? The second objection is implicit and takes the form of questions about the details of the development of the religious imagination: What kinds of family life experiences, what sorts of religious education endeavors, what kind of Sunday sermons are most likely to affect the development of a religious imagination? And what about those who, like Ingmar Bergman, indeed experience the sacred, but experience it as threatening, evil, and ugly?

To the first objection, one must reply that religion is more than emotion. The ecstatic religious experience described by William James is primarily cognitive. The person having the experience *knows*. Similarly, less spectacular religious experiences, the hope-renewing experiences, are also cognitive: they confirm, validate, reinforce the human conviction that there are grounds for hope. Those critics who reduce religious experience to emotionality or, even worse, to sentimentality, do not understand the nature of hope-renewing interludes. Such interludes affect the whole person—however one chooses to define the whole person—and while they have enormous emotional impact, they are more than just feeling.

If one is told, as I have been, that this theory would support the position of the author of The Imitation of Christ, who said that he would rather feel contrition than be able to define it, one must reply that the theory simply has not been understood. If I am told that the theory seems to root religion in feelings about Jesus instead of beliefs and convictions about him, I must again say that the theory has been misunderstood. The hope-renewing experience does not make one merely *feel* that there is loving goodness in the world; one comes away *knowing* that there is. Indeed, the form of knowledge is deeper and more powerful than the rational and discursive knowledge of the catechism and theology textbooks.

A more precise description of the religious experience and the religious imagination would be to say that it is the result of unreflected cognition. The essential human task is not to transform the emotionality and sentimentality of religious experience and religious imagination to mature conviction; the real task is to reflect on the meaning of the conviction that comes with religious experience and is encoded in religious story so that one will be able to articulate and explain the convictions to both oneself and to others. Such an application of reflective intelligence to the imagery in the religious preconscious is imperative, essential, and inevitable, not because the religious imagination is pure emotionality (it surely is not), but because it is the nature of human nature not merely to tell stories but to reflect upon their meaning. Stories, however, are intelligent, artistic creations, not just sentiment, and surely not mere animal imagery. The Church's neoreactionary thinkers (like Professor James Hitchcock, for example) who rail against religious experience as though it were anti-intellectual and devoid of conviction either do not understand the nature of religious experience or are dealing with shallow pseudoreligious experiences.

To the second objection I would note that a model cannot be completely utilized in the first research project it has generated. We hope that this book has demonstrated both the general utility of the model, the capability of survey research/mathematical/ sociology to tease complex findings out of data to show that a sociological theory of the religious imagination works. Stories of God are more powerful than propositions about God, and stories of God are the result of the experiences of loving goodness in human relations rather than of propositional instruction. Further elaboration and refinement of the theory, testing its application in specific human life situations, will require new research specifically designed for such goals. The implications of the theory of the religious imagination are important for Church policy. Such research ought to be funded. It is unreasonable and unrealistic to demand that the first investigation of the religious imagination answer all the questions it raises.

For most of the course of human history, before the invention of the printing press and before universal literacy, before the emergence of philosophical theology and its broad diffusion, religious traditions were passed on from generation to generation by pictures, images, rituals, and stories. In the Middle Ages it was often said, for example, that while there were few schools, religion was taught in festivals, through stained glass windows, paintings and sculpture, folk customs, through the liturgy and through the miracle and morality dramas which were intimately connected with the liturgy. More sophisticated, perhaps, than the storytellers of the primitive tribes, medieval religious educators still used narrative and imaginative methods to pass on the religious tradition.

It has been supposed that the printing press and the school have replaced the dancer, the artist, and the storyteller as key elements is the process of religious education. The classroom teacher trained in propositional instruction, demanding either catechism answers or, more recently, moral development in a baptized version of the Kohlberg moral development paradigm, represents progress over more archaic and less efficient methods for the transmission of religious values.

The research reported in this volume suggests that this assumption may not in fact be accurate. While propositional instruction in a classroom or quasi-classroom environment may well be a useful and even necessary adjunct to the development of the religious imagination, storytelling is still the primary method of passing on a heritage.

The materials presented in the last chapter seem to confirm this position. Mary has received precious little attention in the classroom, the textbook, the modern catechism; yet the Marian imagery flourishes in the minds of postconciliar young people not because they have heard of Mary in the classroom, not because they can distinguish among the various obscure names of new Marian doctrines, but because they have heard the Mary stories, and these stories resonate to the well-nigh universal grace experience of maternity.

The Church seems to have overestimated the importance of propositional instruction and notably underestimated the importance of storytelling in the development of the religious imagination through relationships in which loving goodness is revealed and experienced.

The principal policy conclusion of this book is that the Church must rediscover the religious imagination. It is a broad conclusion indeed, one that sets the agenda for several decades to come. Four preliminary conclusions are drawn:

1. The relationship between the religious imagination in the high arts and religious imagination in ordinary life is delicate, complicated, and by no means fully understood. It seems reasonable to assume, however, that a Church which has no respect for the high arts cannot facilitate the development of the religious imagination among its ordinary people. While Catholicism in the United States is an inheritor of an extraordinary artistic tradition, it can be said quite bluntly that it has absolutely no respect for the high arts. Those things that pass for serious church music or serious church architecture in the United States at the present time, for example, rarely have any artistic merit. American Catholicism is utterly disinterested in poetry, and while it has produced fine novelists (most recently two geniuses in Walker Percy and Joyce Carol Oates), it pays absolutely no attention to such writers—indeed, often viewing them with suspicion. The artist, the craftsman, the performer, such as they may be, are overworked, underpaid, and treated, if not with contempt, then with the supercilious disdain that practical men and women have for those who are really not relevant. Under such circumstances the blossoming talent is frozen to death, and ordinary poetic and artistic gifts that everyone possesses are never given a chance to develop. It is most unlikely that this book or anything else, including a visit from the Angel Gabriel, will shake American Catholicism from its hyper-pragmatic, anti-artistic, anti-intellectual, and anti-imaginative approach to reality.

2. All of us are born poets and storytellers. We have to learn to speak prose and to write nonfiction. The skills of prose and of nonfiction are essential to intelligent human living. Unfortunately, the educational system to which children are subjected in our society tends to stifle the poet and the storyteller. If the religious imagination is important to the human personality, it is only because the whole imagination is important. The development of a mature and healthy imagination is an essential part of education. How imagination may be educated is a problem to which administrators, teachers, and pedagogues might devote considerably more attention than they do. Since Catholic schools are more free from the bureaucratic overload of public schools, they should be able to experiment more ingeniously with the development of the religious imagination—though one trusts that religious imagination does not become a cliché and a buzzword among Catholic educators like "salvation history" and "relevance" and the "Third World" have become in the years since the Council. The research evidence shows that it is high quality religious instruction that contributes to the growth of the religious imagination. One suspects that artsy-craftsy cuteness—which will surely increase should "religious imagination" become a buzzword—doesn't correlate with a gracious story of God at all.

3. The imaginative richness of the Catholic tradition which has served us so well over the last couple of thousand years and continues to serve well, despite the sin of hyper-propositionalized education and the more recent sin of Vatican Council fads, ought to be explored, understood, cherished. The durability and the impact of the Marian imagery simply would not have been believed before our research began. The survival and importance of Mary indicates, perhaps better than anything else, how very different are the religious lives of ordinary people from the concepts of those who write the books, the articles, and the newspaper stories; and how much more these lives are prone to be influenced by the imaginative resources of the Catholic tradition than are the lives, or at least the explicit interests, of the elite. Attitudes on birth control, divorce, abortion, the ordination of women have no effect at all on marital happiness. Stories of Mary do have an effect. The lessons of this finding ought to be self-evident.

4. The Church must not overlook the implications of localism in the religious life of ordinary people. The dominating influences are local and interpersonal—parent, spouse, friend, parish priest. The bishop in his chancery office and the pope in the apostolic palace are far, far away; neither have much importance despite the newspaper headlines they may occasionally receive. If the Church is concerned about developing the religious life and the religious imagination of its people, its major efforts should be directed at facilitating the work of the grass roots religious dynamic. Indeed, the two most obvious dynamics are the quality of the husband and wife intimacy and the quality of Sunday preaching. The Church pays little attention to either. At the Synod of Bishops, in progress as I complete this book, the elected representatives of the bishops of the Church are obsessed with questions of sexual morality, even though most of them now realize that their answers will not be accepted by the ordinary laity and their statements will not be heard. The more subtle questions of the quality of intimacy and motivation for improving that quality in Catholic marriages will not be addressed.

Obsession with the morality of marriage and inattention to the ascetic of it is especially surprising, since the Church has far more riches and resources in its tradition for dealing with the ascetics of intimacy than it does with the morality of intimacy. One American bishop did present an intervention at the Synod on the need for a positive approach to human sexuality, but there is no evidence that the other bishops heard him, much less understood what he said. The document was deemed of such little importance that neither the Catholic nor the secular press paid any attention.

The institutional Church can have only an indirect impact on the marital relationship, but it surely can have a direct impact on the quality of preaching. Indeed, one of the most important challenges facing the Church in the remaining decades of this century will be precisely that of improving the quality of Sunday homilies and other forms of preaching. In the absence of serious efforts in this direction, one would certainly be justified in questioning whether there is any serious commitment at all to improving the effectiveness of the Church or to facilitate the development of the religious imagination.

In brief summary, the present research suggests that we should be more concerned about stories of God and about the places where these stories are told and the relationships within which they are told. We should return, in other words, as the Church must always return, from the high philosophical system to the basic story and from the elaborate administrative bureaucracy to the fireside around which the story is told.

References

Berger, Peter
    1969   *Rumor of Angels*. New York: Doubleday.

Garfinkel, Harold
    1967   *Studies in Ethnomethodology*. Englewood Cliffs, New Jersey: Prentice-Hall.

Geertz, Clifford, ed.
    1967   *Myth, Symbol and Culture*. New York: Norton, (Daedalus Series).

Goffman, Erving
    1974   *Frame Analysis: An Essay on the Organization of Experience*. Cambridge, Massachusetts: Harvard University Press.

Greeley, Andrew
    1981   *Religion: A Secular Theory*. New York: The Free Press.
    1977   *The Mary Myth: On the Femininity of God*. New York: Seabury.
    1976   *Catholic Schools in a Declining Church*. Kansas City: Sheed, Andrews and McMeel.

Hardy, Alistair
    1974   *The Challenge of Chance: A Mass Experiment in Telepathy and Its Outcomes*. New York: Oxford University Press.

Hogan, Dennis P.
    1976   "Differentials and Trends in Structure of Family of Origin." Paper read at the 71st Annual Meeting, American Sociological Association, New York.

James, William
    1936   *The Varieties of Religious Experience*. New York: Random House (Modern Library).

King, Morton B. and Richard A. Hunt
    1975   "Measuring the Religious Variable." *Journal for the Scientific Study of Religion*, 14:13-22.

Krump, John M.
    1979   *Youth and the Church*. Chicago: Thomas More Press.

Kubie, Lawrence
    1961   *Neurotic Distortion and the Creative Process*. New York: Farrar, Straus and Giroux.

Levi-Strauss, Claude
    1979   *Myth and Meaning*. Toronto: University of Toronto Press.
    1973   *From Honey to Ashes: An Introduction to the Science of Mythology*. New York: Harper and Row.

MacQuarrie,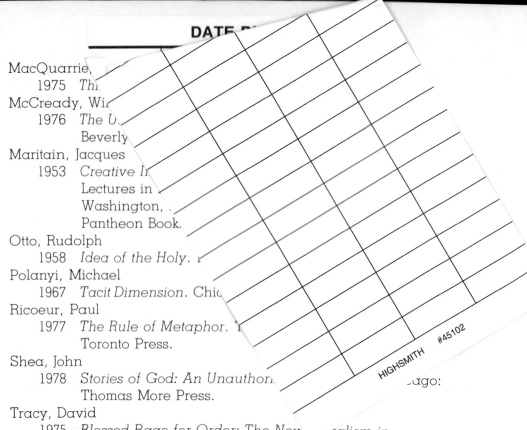
    1975   Thi

McCready, Wi
    1976   The U.
            Beverly

Maritain, Jacques
    1953   Creative In
            Lectures in
            Washington,
            Pantheon Book.

Otto, Rudolph
    1958   Idea of the Holy.

Polanyi, Michael
    1967   Tacit Dimension. Chic

Ricoeur, Paul
    1977   The Rule of Metaphor.
            Toronto Press.

Shea, John
    1978   Stories of God: An Unauthor   _ago:
            Thomas More Press.

Tracy, David
    1975   Blessed Rage for Order: The New   _ralism in
            Theology. New York: Seabury Press.

Verba, Sidney and Norman H. Nie
    1972   Participation in America. New York: Harper and Row.

Warner, Marina
    1976   Alone of All Her Sex: The Myth and Cult of the
            Virgin Mary. New York: Knopf.

Wuthnow, Robert
    1976   The Consciousness Reformation. Berkeley, California:
            University of California Press.